Behind the Hedge

Where our food comes from
A pocket guide to British farming

Nicola de Pulford and John Hitchins

© Nicola de Pulford and John Hitchins, 2012

Published by Sigma Leisure – an imprint of
Sigma Press, Stobart House, Pontyclerc, Penybanc Road
Ammanford, Carmarthenshire SA18 3HP

British Library Cataloguing in Publication Data

A CIP record for this book is available from the British Library

ISBN: 978-1-85058-919-8

Typesetting and Design by: Sigma Press, Ammanford, Carms

Photographs: © Nicola de Pulford, except photographs credited on page 255

Cover photographs: © Nicola de Pulford, unless stated otherwise;
(left to right) above: Crossbred ewe and lamb; Ploughing; Ear of barley
middle: Two sows © Mr & Mrs Joel, Framfield Farm; Rape flowers; Cutting corn
with horses at vintage rally modern
below: Salad landscape © Leafy Salads Association; Maran; Child and goat kids

Printed by: Akcent Media Ltd

Disclaimer: The information in this book is given in good faith and is believed to be correct at the time of publication.

Contents

About the Authors

Nicola de Pulford is a farmer, a photographer and best-selling writer. Brought up on a mixed farm in Wiltshire, she ran the farm with her sister from the age of 17. She now farms in Devon keeping sheep, goats, poultry, ducks and growing a variety of vegetables for the local market. She publishes the Naked Farmers's Calendar.

John Hitchins has been a journalist, a greengrocer and, for a brief period, worked on a farm in India. He has lived in South Devon for the past 25 years surrounded by some of Britain's most beautiful farmland but knowing little of what is growing and grazing around him. He has written this book to overcome his own ignorance and that of millions like him.

Introduction

This book is for everybody who is interested in the food we eat, the way it is produced and the land it comes from.

In Britain, farmers often appear to be an endangered species. Most people live in cities and shop in supermarkets, and it is little wonder that their knowledge of farming is confined to an occasional episode of Emmerdale on TV.

Thanks to David Attenborough, many of us are more familiar with a hump-backed whale or an orangutan than the pig or hen which provides our breakfast bacon-and-eggs.

Because so much of what we eat is processed, packaged or frozen we can forget where it comes from. The food chain has now grown so long it is easy to lose sight of the farmer at the other end.

But despite urban sprawl, Britain is still a rural country. And most of our green and pleasant land is still farmed. Beautiful as it may be, our countryside is almost all man-made. It looks like it is because, in order to survive and flourish, we have shaped the land to enclose animals and cultivate crops.

Our surnames should remind us. The Shepherd, Miller. Swain and Smith families may live in Manchester, London or Glasgow now, but their ties to the land were once strong.

Behind the Hedge is for those who want to know more about the land and those who

Our green and pleasant land is man-made

farm it. It is an easy-to-follow guide which will help you identify in their natural environment the crops, fruit and farm animals which we consume as food.

Many children are so accustomed to eating prepared and packaged food that they do not know what a carrot, a leek or a green bean look like in their natural form. Even in the countryside some children can be sadly unaware of the food that grows around them.

When a new, "healthier" meal service was introduced at the primary school which our own children attended, the cook was horrified to discover that half of the children did not recognise a boiled potato when it was served to them instead of the chips and waffles they were accustomed to !

Through the car window we see a blue or yellow field in the distance without knowing what crop is growing there. Very few of us can recognise common breeds of cattle and sheep, let alone goats, geese, chickens and pigs. And everyday farming terms like heifer, bullock, bantam or silage might as well be Greek to most city dwellers.

This guidebook describes clearly in words and pictures the crops, animals, farmland, buildings, machinery and wildlife that characterise the British countryside.

We hope you use it and enjoy it.

Nicola de Pulford and John Hitchins

Growing crops

Once upon a time everything we ate in Britain was grown in Britain. Now more than half our food is imported, either because it is cheaper or because some products, such as avocados, mangos or oranges, cannot be grown here. Yet even when crops flourish in Britain, we still import more than we grow.

We only produce twenty per cent of the tomatoes we eat, for example. And even at the height of the English apple season the home-grown crop still only makes up a third of the apples on supermarket shelves.

Many of the crops that we do grow in Britain don't end up on our plates at all. At least, not in a form we would recognise.

They are fed to the cattle, sheep and pigs whose meat we consume every day.

Kale, maize, beet, turnips, barley and oats, for example, form a vital part of the diet of livestock, especially in the winter. They may be grazed in the field, cut and stored for feeding to animals later, or turned into silage or cattle cake. We do eat these crops ourselves but not in anything like the quantities that animals do.

And then there is grass. This is the most important agricultural crop of all. We don't eat it ourselves, of course, but it is the most important component of the diet of the ten million cattle and thirty million sheep in the UK. Seventy per cent of farmland in the country is grass.

Harvesting maize with a forage harvester

Grassland may be permanent pasture or sown periodically as part of a rotation system, when it is known as "leys" which may be grazed from two to five years before being ploughed and replanted with other crops. Leys are an essential part of the farming cycle – especially organic farming - because the animals that graze on the grass return nutrients to the soil in the form of manure which is then used by the crops in the next rotation. Once the soil is exhausted, the ley is resown with grass seed and the process of fertilisation begins again.

All crops are seasonal and the nature of the British climate requires farmers to make the most of the daylight, sunshine and warmer temperatures of the summer. Cereals may be planted in the winter or spring, but they are all harvested in late summer or autumn. The season for fruit and vegetable picking is much longer, from early new potatoes and asparagus to later maturing apples and root vegetables, with carrots and leeks, for example, being picked all year.

Most cereals are planted by drilling seed directly into the soil, but where there is a risk that seeds will not germinate consistently then they may be propagated under cover and planted out as seedlings or small plants. Cauliflowers and strawberries are raised in this way.

The east of Britain, especially East Anglia, remains the main production area for grain and vegetables. But farmers all over the country respond yearly to changes in the demand for different crops and the prices on offer. Hence the appearance (and disappearance) of fields of yellow rape (for oil) and elephant grass (as fuel for power stations) all over the country as the market has changed.

One problem for farmers is that while they may expect high prices for their crops when they plant them, those prices may fall by the time the crops are harvested. This is why so many enter into fixed price contracts for their products, even when that is below the "spot price" available at any one time. Many bigger fruit and vegetable growers have entered into long-term relationships with the major supermarkets, either directly or via large packers and processors.

Farmers looking for a niche market may decide to grow fruit, vegetables or herbs to meet a small but clearly identified demand. Where possible they will sell directly to the end customer, cutting out the wholesaler

Collecting peas for freezing

Bicycling through Thanet Earth

Using a specialist rig to harvest carrots

or retailer, thus retaining more of the end price for themselves. Organic vegetable growers have been at the forefront of this trend, selling to individual customers – and increasing their margins – through door-to-door delivery. One of the largest of these, Riverford Farm, is a pioneer of this "veg box" scheme (see page 65).

And, of course, through the increasing growth and sophistication of farm shops, hundreds of farmers are becoming their own retailer.

In this book we have tried to avoid terms like "arable" or "horticulture" because all growers of crops, fruit and vegetables are engaged in the same task of earning a living from the land.

The term arable usually applies to the large scale production of cereals, oilseeds, root vegetables and brassicas, while horticulture is reserved for the more intensive growing

> There are five factors for the farmer to consider in choosing which crops to grow: the nature of the soil, the climate, altitude, aspect and the market for the crop. To this can be added the availability of artificial protection such as glasshouses or polytunnels which has made it possible to grow higher value crops such as strawberries or asparagus more reliably and for a longer period.

of vegetables, fruit and flowers, often where the crop is protected by glasshouses or polytunnels.

And even though horticulture takes up only three per cent of the land available for crops in the UK, the value of sales of fruit and vegetables is £15 billion a year. Annual sales of Britain's biggest crop, wheat, which takes up ten times as much land, are just over £20 billion.

Vegetables like tomatoes and cucumbers are also being grown on a large scale in ways which would have been considered impossible a few years ago. Huge glasshouses, like those at Thanet Earth in Kent, have been built for these so called "protected" crops to extend the season and increase output. They are not raised in soil any more, or even compost. They are planted in rockwool – similar to the material used in roof insulation – with supplies of water, warmth and nutrients monitored by sensors and controlled by computer.

It may be called horticulture, but in financial terms their operations are bigger than all but the most extensive arable farms.

Despite these dramatic changes in the production of some fruit and vegetables, most crops are still grown on family farms in traditional ways, and in this chapter we look at the most important ones.

Apples

We only grow about 15% of the apples we eat, but many apple orchards have been replanted in recent years and supermarkets are now stocking more English varieties. Half our apples are grown for cider.

Gala, Braeburn and Cox's Orange Pippin are among the most common varieties of dessert apple grown in the UK and traditional apples such as Russet and Worcester Pearmain are still grown. Pippin is an old English word derived from the French for seedling and the apple is thought to be named after a Yorkshire brewer, Richard Cox.

Cider apples have more tannin and acid and are not good for eating, but they can be harvested by machine because damage to the fruit is not so critical as with dessert apples. Most cider apples are grown in Herefordshire and Somerset. Apples are vulnerable to frost, and need to be sprayed to eliminate a number of pests and diseases.

What they look like

Trees grown for dessert apples tend to be smaller than cider apple trees, and grow to 20 feet or more. Orchards are full of pale pink and white blossom in late April and early May and the tiny fruitlets appear on

Malus domestica
Perennial
Grafted onto exisitng root stock
Harvested: September and October
Life cycle: About 20 years

Most Prolific Areas of Cultivation:
Kent, Sussex, Herefordshire, Somerset

some trees in June. Most of the crop is harvested in September and October.

How they are used

About one third of the apples we eat between August and April are home-grown, and this proportion has risen as supermarkets have increased the range of English apples they stock. Half the Bramley crop is sliced and diced for food processing (eg. prepared apple pies) or the catering trade. Mass produced apple juice is not made from British apples.

Did you know ?
- Apple pips contain traces of cyanide but they can be eaten without ill-effects
- Apples originated in the Middle East and only became established in Britain when Henry the Eighth planted orchards in Kent with varieties from around the world
- One of our most popular apples, the Granny Smith, is not grown in the UK

Apple blossom

Foxwhelp cider apples

Artichokes

They may share the same name, but the Globe artichoke is a member of the thistle family and the Jerusalem artichoke is a root vegetable. Both are delicious.

Globe artichokes with their large, round, leafy heads and spiky leaves, resemble a large thistle. Most varieties grown in the UK are similar to the Roscoff artichoke grown in Northern Brittany.

They can produce heads for six years before they need to be dug up and replanted. The heads are often cut in June, enabling a second crop to be harvested in August or September.

What they look like

The stem and leaves of Jerusalem artichokes (helianthus tuberosus) can be trained to act as a windbreak but it is their underground tubers that are lifted from October.

They are members of the sunflower family – they have a yellow flower themselves - and their name is thought to derive from girasole, the Italian name for sunflowers. They have nothing to do with Jerusalem and, like sunflowers, can grow up to eight feet.

Like globe artichokes, they can be left in the ground for several years to reshoot and grow again. They are dug up using a modified potato harvester from November to January.

Both varieties are grown commercially in Lincolnshire, and they are also a popular vegetable with organic growers.

Just to make things complicated there is also a Chinese artichoke (Stachys affinis) which is also a tuber, but technically a member of the mint family.

How they are used

The leaves of globe artichokes are peeled and sucked – often with a lemon or vinaigrette

Cynara Cadunculus (Globe Artichoke)
Harvested: August to September

Helianthus Tuberosus (Jerusalem Artichoke)
Harvested: October to January

Most Prolific Areas of Cultivation: Lincolnshire

Globe Artichoke

Jerusalem Artichokes

dressing – by those who love their delicate flavour. Jerusalem artichokes are normally cooked like potatoes or turned into a soup.

Asparagus

The first green vegetable of the British season and the one considered by many chefs to be the most delicate and delicious of them all.

Asparagus Officinalis
Perennial
Grown from: Rhizomes known as 'crowns'
Harvested: May and June
Life cycle: About 10 years

Most Prolific Areas of Cultivation:
Vale of Evesham and Lincolnshire

Traditionally, the season for British-grown asparagus starts on St. George's Day (April 23rd) and lasts for eight weeks. It needs a warm soil (10 to 12C) which is why the first asparagus usually comes from Cornwall, moving to Scotland for the end of the season.

Most asparagus is grown naturally on light, sandy soils but some growers are using polytunnels and even underground heating to bring the season forward. The crop takes two years to establish. The green stalks, or spears, have to be cut by hand and need to be eaten quickly before the sugars in the plant turn to starch.

Did you know ?
- Asparagus is considered by many to be an aphrodisiac
- The leading exporter of the crop is Peru

What it looks like
Because the plants are large, rows of asparagus are some distance apart. The spears emerge quickly once the soil warms up, and are cut from just beneath the ground. In hot weather they need to be cut every day. The cutters use a tractor driven rig, or individual asparagus "buggies," to aid the harvesting process.

After mid June spears are left to grow into ferns, which return nutrients to the crown and ensure a healthy crop for the following year. Ferns are left to grow until September and can reach three metres before being cut down.

White asparagus, popular in France, is covered with soil to keep it blanched before picking and never sees the light of day. Relatives of asparagus can be found in the wild.

How it is used
Almost all asparagus in Britain is sold as a fresh vegetable, with ferns going to florists.

Young asparagus spears

Asparagus fern at the end of the season

Barley

Closely associated with malt liquor, this grain has become personified in poetry and prose as John Barleycorn, the cause of drunkenness. It is the UK's second most important cereal crop, and most of it is grown for animal feed.

Hordeum Vulgare
Annual
Grown from: Seed
Harvested: July and August
Rotation: One year in four

Most Prolific Areas of Cultivation:
North and West of the UK

Descended from meadow barley or wall barley, whose bristly spikes, called awns, children use to throw like darts, barley was one of the earliest cereals to be grown for food and flourishes in a wide range of climates. It grows in dry soils throughout the country, and is often the main arable crop in the north and west of the country where it is difficult to grow wheat.

What it looks like

Barley grows to the same height as wheat (about a metre) but it droops so that the ears hang down with very long whiskers – the awns. A field of barley thus has a more windswept appearance and is easily identifiable on breezy days when "waves" blow through the crop.

Three varieties are cultivated, each with a different number of kernel rows in the head. Two-row barley is traditionally used in English beers and six-row barley is preferred by American and German brewers. Four-row barley is not suitable for brewing.

How it is used

In the UK one third of the barley crop (mainly Spring barley) is used to make beer, whiskey and malted drinks and two thirds goes into cattle food. Barley flour does not "rise" well because it is low in gluten, and this is why it is not often used to make bread.

Barley is popular in soups and stews. Barley flakes – grains which have been pressed and flattened - are often added to muesli and other breakfast cereals. Pot barley, also known as Scotch barley, has the outer husk and some of the bran removed. Pearl barley has the outer husk bran removed before being steamed, rounded and polished.

Barley straw is widely used as bedding and fodder for livestock.

Did you know ?
- A stack of barley is known as a barley mow, after which many pubs are named
- Barley sugar is not made of barley but Horlicks is !
- The word barn comes from the Old English for barley store

Broccoli

Broccoli has become more popular in recent years at the expense of cauliflower and is now the most valuable UK crop in the cabbage family. It is also known as calabrese after the Calabria region of Italy where it is common.

Brassica oleracea italica
Annual
Grown from: Seed or transplanted
Harvested: May to November (Calabrese)
January to May (Purple Sprouting Broccoli)

Most Prolific Areas of Cultivation: Throughout the UK

Green calabrese broccoli can be very sensitive to wet and cold, which is why it is strange that two popular varieties are called Marathon and Ironman. It has rapidly become one of the most popular green vegetables, although purple sprouting broccoli is enjoying a renaissance.

What it looks like

As demand for broccoli has risen, some growers are planting under glass in February or March to produce an earlier crop. Most broccoli is sown from March until August in open fields, although early in the season the new plants may be protected by fleece or plastic. The crop requires high levels of moisture and most fields need to be irrigated.

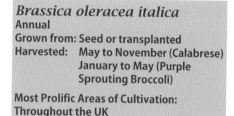

Calabrese broccoli

The edible portion of broccoli is the bright green stem and head of green flower buds known as a "spear." When it is ready to harvest, the broccoli spear should be 60 – 100 mm wide and 150 mm long. It is surrounded by leaves. Spears are easily damaged if there are summer hailstorms.

The hardier purple sprouting broccoli has more heads than calabrese and many thin stalks. It is harvested in the spring. A white sprouting broccoli is a variety of its own, not a purple version that has gone wrong!

Romanesco broccoli has one large head, similar to a cauliflower, with a spiky, lime green appearance

How it is used

Broccoli is usually boiled or steamed, but it can be eaten raw. It is popular as an hors d'oeuvre with dips, an ingredient in salads or topped with cheese.

Purple sprouting broccoli

Brussels Sprouts

Brussels Sprouts are sometimes sold on the stem to preserve freshness

Brassica oleracea
Annual
Grown from: Seed and transplanted
Harvested: August to April
Rotation: One year in four

Most Prolific Areas of Cultivation:
Lincolnshire, Lancashire, Yorkshire, Scotland

Children hate them. Grown-ups love them. These miniature cabbages are one of the most popular green vegetables in Britain, despite their Belgian connections.

It is thought they were cultivated in Roman times but the modern sprout was first grown in large quantities in the area around Brussels in Belgium in the Middle Ages. They spread across Europe during the First World War. Brussels sprouts are rich in Vitamin C.

What they look like
Sprouts are planted out as modules in April or May when they are eight or nine inches high. Instead of branching out, the buds on the stem of this member of the cabbage family remain compact and grow to reach one or two inches in diameter.

Early varieties of sprouts, such as the Oliver, are harvested from August, with later varieties being cut throughout the winter. The most popular variety grown is Maximus which is harvested during October and November.

Each stalk, which is about a metre high when cut, produces between forty and eighty sprouts weighing about a kilogram. The sprout harvester cuts through the stalks at ground level using a horizontal blade and the operator feeds the stalk into a stripper which removes the sprouts with rotating knives. The stalks are ejected and later ploughed back into the field.

How they are used
Almost all brussels sprouts grown in the UK are sold as fresh vegetables.

Did you know ?
- If brussels sprouts are overcooked they smell of sulphur, which is probably why children dislike them
- It has been suggested that sprouts protect against colon cancer because they contain sinigrin (the chemical which smells of sulphur)

Newly-planted sprouts

Cabbage

The traditional "April" cabbage variety

Brassica oleracea capitata
Biennial
Grown from: Seed and transplanted
Harvested: All year
Rotation: One year in four

Most Prolific Areas of Cultivation:
Lincolnshire, West Cornwall, Kent, Lancashire

Cabbage comes in many different shapes and sizes. Spring greens, despite their name, are available in different parts of the country throughout the year. Summer and autumn primo cabbages are "hearted" and cabbages picked in winter include January King, Savoy and red cabbage. Because they are tolerant of a range of different soils, cabbages can be grown in most parts of the country

What they look like

The common round "white" cabbage (really light green), known as Dutch white cabbage, and red cabbage (really purple) used to be known as Drumheads. Because of the flattened nature of the head of overlapping, smooth leaves, they need to be planted well apart.

Savoy cabbages, with their dark, curly leaves, are a hardier variety and although they can be harvested all year round are most popular in winter. Spring Greens, without a heart, are now produced all the year round.

White and red cabbage may be stored in refrigerated or controlled atmosphere stores for up to 10 months.

How are they used

Cabbages are sold throughout the year as a green (or red!) vegetable and they are also used to feed animals in the winter. Cabbage is the main ingredient in coleslaw and sauerkraut, and is widely used in soups such as borscht.

Rows of newly-transplanted cabbages

Did you know ?
- The name cabbage comes from caboche, the old French word for head
- The Chinese produce twice as much cabbage as the rest of the world
- Boiling cabbage too long is what causes the "school dinners" smell

Carrots

The British grow and eat more carrots than any other fresh vegetable and half the nation's children list them as their favourite. And, yes, they do help you see in the dark.

Different varieties and growing techniques ensure a fresh home-grown supply all year. Carrots prefer well-drained sandy or peat soils. They need to be irrigated to achieve a good yield, and to prevent the sandy soils blowing away, carrot seeds are often drilled with barley or mustard which acts as a protective cover crop.

Did you know ?
- The carrot takes its name from a pigment called carotenoid which gives the vegetable its orange colour.
- Carrots are thought to have originated in Afghanistan, where they were originally purple
- The beta-carotene in carrots is converted by the body into vitamin A, which is important for healthy vision

Early season carrots are sown in the winter and protected with plastic or fleece. Another crop is sown in spring and harvested from August. Late carrots are sown in early summer and harvested from December to May. They are covered in straw to protect them during the winter.

In the early part of the season carrots are harvested by machines which undercut the crop and lift the carrots out by their foliage. These "top lifters" normally work at night. When the foliage is weaker and the roots strong, they are lifted out by "share harvesters."

What they look like
Carrots come in all shapes and sizes, but the supermarkets require straight,

Daucus Carota
Annual
Grown from: Seed
Harvested: Anytime of the year
Rotation: One year in five

Most Prolific Areas of Cultivation:
The Fens, Lancashire, Norfolk, Nottinghamshire,Scotland

undamaged roots with a good colour. Nantes type carrots are cylindrical and Chantenay are conical. At harvest time, when the carrots are lifted mechanically, a small amount of the orange carrot is visible above the ground beneath the fern like leaves (see photo above).

How they are used
Carrots are sold as fresh vegetables in supermarkets and greengrocers throughout the year. They are also canned, frozen and processed.

Cauliflower

In Mark Twain's view, "cauliflower is nothing but cabbage with a college education." The amount of cauliflower grown in the UK is falling, and we now only produce half of what we eat.

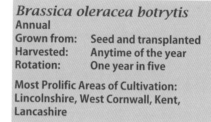

Brassica oleracea botrytis
Annual
Grown from: Seed and transplanted
Harvested: Anytime of the year
Rotation: One year in five

Most Prolific Areas of Cultivation:
Lincolnshire, West Cornwall, Kent, Lancashire

Cauliflower comes from the Latin words caulis (stalk) and floris (flower) because it is made up of tiny florets on clusters of stalks. The florets, which are normally white, but can be green or purple, are known as the "curd." The distribution of the crop varies from year to year according to the price that farmers can achieve. Winter varieties are common in the mild climates of West Cornwall and in Thanet, Kent, where cauliflowers may be grown in rotation with early potatoes.

What they look like

Cauliflowers are transplanted into the field as plants grown in module trays under glass. Supermarkets insist on evenly sized and shaped heads which are as white as possible. Its wrapping of light green leaves makes the cauliflower the closest there is to a "pre-packaged" vegetable but as much as a third of the crop may be rejected before harvest as not "perfect" enough.

The vegetable must be protected against pests such as the cabbage root fly and this requires pesticides or, in the case of organic growers, covering the crop with fleece or mesh during egg-laying periods.

How they are used

The curd is normally cooked as a table vegetable, but the leaves can also be eaten. Cauliflower is often pickled, and is a principal ingredient in piccalilli. Among the most popular uses are cauliflower cheese and the Indian dish Aloo Gobi.

Cauliflowers must be hand-picked

The whiter the head the better

Did you know ?
- Three quarters of the world's cauliflowers are grown in India and China
- Green cauliflower is sometimes called broccoflower; if it has spiky heads it is called Romanesco Broccoli
- Boxers, wrestlers and rugby players frequently suffer from damaged or "cauliflower" ears

Celeriac

Apium graveolens rapaceum

Not widely grown in Britain until recently, this ugly but nutritious root vegetable has become popular as celebrity chefs have sung its praises. It is grown mainly on the silt soils of Lincolnshire.

Unlike celery, its close relative, celeriac is grown for its knobby edible root, which is

A knobbly root with a delicious flavour

used as a raw or cooked vegetable. It is sometimes called celery root or turnip rooted celery. Celeriac is very vulnerable to the soil-borne disease sclerotinia, which can destroy the crop in the ground or under refrigeration.

After it is planted out in May, celeriac grows steadily producing a deep green bushy foliage. An adapted potato harvester is used to undercut the crop when it is ready. Although it is taken out of the ground in the autumn, home-grown celeriac can be kept in refrigerated stores and made available all year.

In France it is almost all used to make celeri remoulade, a salad of chopped celeriac dressed with mayonnaise and mustard. In Britain it is usually cut into smaller pieces and roasted, or mixed with mashed potatoes or swede.

Celery

Apium Graveolans

Celery needs plenty of deep fertile soil, water and sunshine, and a long growing season with cool nights. The rich, deep Fenland soils of Cambridgeshire are ideal and provide much of the home-grown celery consumed in the UK.

Celery is grown from seed in greenhouses and transplanted to fields at the end of February when the celery plants are 4-6 inches tall. Harvesting starts in June and continues until November. The fastest growing celery is ready to harvest in 12 weeks.

Harvesting is labour-intensive because the crop is normally cut by hand using a specially shaped knife and packed in the field using mobile rigs. The celery then needs to be stored in temperature controlled conditions for delivery to retailers the following day.

A later crop of winter celery was traditionally grown in England for the Christmas market, and this had to be "banked up" to blanch it and protect it from frost. This Christmas celery, which is whiter than normal celery and has a nuttier, sweeter taste, has been re-introduced by some growers.

Trimming celery before packing

Cherries

Prunus Avium

Only a tiny proportion of the cherries we eat are grown in Britain, but newer orchards are proving more productive and yields are slowly increasing.

The planting of smaller trees which can be netted to protect the fruit from birds and hail has halted the rapid decline in cherry orchards. It has also made it possible to pick the cherries from below, rather than having to use large ladders.

Varieties include Kordia, Penny, Summersun and Sasha. They are grafted on to dwarf rootstock.

Although the area of cherry orchards is only slowly increasing, the volume of fruit produced is rapidly rising because of much larger yields.

Chicory

Cichorium Intybus

A plant with two uses. The leaves are turned into a salad or cooked vegetable and the roots can be made into a form of coffee.

Grown from seed and harvested all year round, chicory is known elsewhere as endive or witloof and it is an unusual vegetable. Seeds are drilled in May and at any time from November the roots are dug up and kept in storage at minus two degrees to stop them growing any more.

A small quantity are taken out of storage each week and the roots "forced" by putting them in a nutrient solution in a dark room. Under this hydroponic process the blanched leaves grow in two or three weeks and are cut for sale throughout the year. Red and white varieties are available.

All chicory grown in the UK – mainly in Lincolnshire - is sold for its fresh leaves, or chicons, which have a slightly bitter taste. But for many years the dried and roasted chicory root was turned into a familiar coffee substitute called Camp coffee, which is still available. The chopped roots are now used as animal feed.

Clover

Clovers are part of the Legume family of plants which can convert nitrogen from the air. This is known as 'nitrogen fixation' and has long been used in crop rotation systems to improve the soil

What it looks like

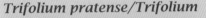

Trifolium pratense/Trifolium repens
Perennial sometimes biennial herb
Grown from: Seed
Harvested: May to August

Most Prolific Areas of Cultivation:
Commonly found throughout the UK

Red and white clover can be used to feed animals and as a green manure

Red clover is a short lived perennial that survives for two to four years. It grows upright and has a deep tap root. The leaves have three leaflets and the rose-purple coloured flower heads are comprised of many flowers.

White clover flower heads also have many flowers with leaves like the red. They are longer lived and have multi-branched creeping stems (stolons).

How it is used

Clover is extensively grown as a fodder crop for livestock and poultry. It is planted in pastures with grass and can be grazed or cut as silage or for hay. It is also used as a cover crop and as green manure to improve soil condition. The root system of clovers improves the soil structure, suppresses weeds and boosts nitrogen levels in the pasture. It is rich in protein so has a high feed value for livestock, although it has the potential to cause 'bloat' if overfed.

Did you know ?
- Red clover is often known as 'bee bread' because bees love the nectar.
- Rare four leaf clovers were worn to ward off evil spirits and bring good luck

Courgettes

(and marrow, squash, pumpkin, and gourds)

Courgettes are essentially immature versions of marrows which are picked continuously before they have a chance to develop. In Britain they are the most popular members of the gourd family, and are widely grown in the rich fenlands of Cambridgeshire

Courgettes or zucchinis, as the Americans call them, are small marrows ("courge" is the French for marrow and "zucca" the Italian). They have become much more popular than full-grown marrows, especially among children.

Squash is the American Indian term covering most summer (fresh) and winter (stored) members of the cucurbit or "gourd" family. . Summer cucurbits are marrows, courgettes and gem squashes.

Winter squashes are essentially storage squashes grown to full maturity, usually picked after the skin has set. A pumpkin is a winter storage squash. So are gourds.

Did you know ?
- Courgette flowers make delicious omelettes
- Europe's largest pumpkin grower is at Spalding in Lincolnshire and grows two million a year
- Butternut is the easiest squash to peel

What they look like
Marrows, courgettes and squashes are mainly grown out of doors. They trail along the ground, produce yellow flowers (which can be eaten) and go on cropping for several weeks. Once their leaves die back, squashes and pumpkins make a bright red or orange display across the field before harvesting.

Cucurbita Pepo
Annual
Grown from: Seed then transplanted
Harvested: Summer and Autumn
Rotation: One year in three

Most Prolific Areas of Cultivation:
The Fens

A young pumpkin

How they are used
Courgettes are sold primarily as fresh vegetables and used in stir fries, curries and salads. Marrows often go into pickles, pumpkins into soups and the best flavoured squash, such as butternut or Crown Prince, can be eaten as a fresh vegetable or in soups. If cooked correctly, the skins of Pumpkins and all Squashes can be edible, but many varieties are difficult to peel.

Courgettes and their flowers

Cucumber

Cucumia Sativus
Annual
Grown from: Seed
Harvested: January to November

Most Prolific Areas of Cultivation:
Yorkshire, Kent (Thanet) and Essex (Lea Valley)

nutrients controlled by computer. The high value of the crop – one hectare of glasshouse can produce an annual crop worth £350,000 – justifies the heavy investment needed as long as the cucumbers stay healthy and the yield remains high.

What they look like

Plants are usually propagated by specialist plants raisers in November/December and transferred to production glasshouses from December through to August. Three crops are normally grown each year to maintain quality and a steady output.

Cucumbers are trained to climb up strings or wires about two metres high and the side shoots allowed to cascade downwards in "cordons." Yellow female flowers with a very small cucumber behind them are produced at every leaf and these grow into the cucumbers we eat. Each plant produces from 25 to 50 cucumbers, depending on the time of year. Only the female plant is grown and produces cucumbers.

Research shows that if glasshouses are lit at night cucumbers can be produced 52 weeks a year, but the price paid for cucumbers does not presently justify the extra costs of lighting and energy.

How they are used

Most cucumbers are sold as fresh vegetables, with some processed for pickles and soups.

Demand for cucumbers has always been high in Britain. They are now almost all grown in heated glasshouses, including the giant Thanet Earth in Kent

Like tomatoes, most cucumbers are grown in rockwool, with the supply of water and

Did you know ?
- The cucumber is 95% water, which is why it is so low in calories
- Enclosing a seed and developing from a flower, a cucumber is technically a fruit
- Pickled cucumbers sold to eat with fish and chips are sometimes called "wallies" in the north of England

Elephant Grass

Grown primarily as an energy crop to burn in power stations, the giant grass is seen by some as a threat to the traditional farming landscape. A close relative of sugar cane, it is a favourite food of elephants, hence the name.

Miscanthus giganteus
Perennial
Grown from: Rhizome
Harvested: March and April
Life cycle: 15 years

Most Prolific Areas of Cultivation:
Throughout the UK

What if looks like

Foliage resembles an overgrown bamboo

An overgrown bamboo crowned by a feathery silver-coloured foliage, it grows to a height of ten feet in dense clumps. Leaves are two to three feet long with razor-sharp edges, making elephant grass difficult to penetrate. The grass reproduces through r h i z o m e s , underground root systems which take time to grow and produce erect, robust stems similar to thin bamboo cane. In Northern Europe elephant grass does not flower.

Where you find it

Until recently only a few hundred acres of elephant grass could be found in Britain. But it is now being grown by a large number of farmers throughout the UK to help meet the Government's target of generating more of our energy from renewable sources.

How it is used

Elephant grass is burned to generate electricity in biomass power stations. A typical yield of 12 tons from one hectare can produce enough energy to replace 36 barrels of oil. Biomass crops like elephant grass are "carbon neutral". As they grow they absorb carbon dioxide from the atmosphere, releasing the same amount when they are burnt.

The fibre can also be used in the manufacture of paper and insulation board, and the chopped straw is used for animal bedding.

Did you know ?
• Miscanthus is not the same as the elephant grass grown in Africa (pennisetum purpureum) which is also known as Napier or Uganda grass

Miscanthus is unusual in being harvested in the Spring

Field Beans

Beans and peas are important arable crops because they "fix" nitrogen in the soil and provide a valuable break in the rotation system which restores the fertility of fields after they have been planted with cereals.

Vicia Faba
Annual
Grown from: Seed
Harvested: August and September
Rotation: One year in six

Most Prolific Areas of Cultivation:
Throughout the UK

One type of broad bean is known as "field beans" to farmers. They are an important source of food for livestock because they have a high protein content and reduce farmers' dependence on imported soya bean feed.

They can be planted in the autumn or spring, and because the seeds have their own nutrient source they can be spread over fields – or "broadcast" – and ploughed into the soil, as well as being precision drilled.

What they look like

Beans that have been sown in the autumn will come into flower in early May. They have square stems and large white flowers with dark purple centres. Some varieties of bean resemble elongated peas, others are kidney shaped.

Beans can be picked early for human consumption, but they are ready for harvesting as animal feed when the leaves and pods have turned black, and the beans inside are white and dry.

How they are used

Most field beans are "combined" and turned into food for livestock, being mixed and milled into feed compounds.

Younger broad beans are harvested by large machines called pea viners and frozen or sold as fresh vegetables.

Some beans are exported, especially to the Middle East, and smaller varieties can be used as pigeon feed.

Flowers

The British spend two billion pounds a year on cut flowers and pot plants but only ten per cent are home-grown.

Flowers grown commercially in the UK include freesia, iris, roses, chrysanthemums, narcissi, daffodils, tulips, lisianthus, lilies, poinsettia and alstroemeria. There is also a sizeable business producing houseplants such as African violets, begonias and potted bulbs.

> **Did you know ?**
> • Carnations, roses and lilies are the three best-selling cut flowers in the UK
> • The UK is the world's largest producer of cut-flower daffodils

Most flowers are grown out of doors, with some added protection from plastic covers. Chrysanthemums are grown outside for the main season – August until October – and raised in glasshouses for the Christmas market.

Iris

Garlic

Hand hoeing garlic

Used as a food, a medicine and – in some Asian countries – as an aphrodisiac, garlic is one of the most widely used flavourings throughout the world. The leading producers are China and India.

Garlic is a hardy plant and is grown in several parts of the United Kingdom,

Allium sativum

where the cloves are planted in the autumn and harvested in late Spring. A member of the onion family, it grows to about 60 cms tall. The bulbs are made up of small cloves, and both are covered with a white papery coat.

It needs a well-drained and well-worked soil to prevent rotting and allow the bulbs to swell without being constrained. Garlic can be planted mechanically, but elephant garlic, which produce bigger bulbs and command a higher price, must be hand planted with the clove the right way up. Garlic should not be planted in the same ground more than one year in six.

The biggest specialist garlic farm in the UK is near Sandown on the Isle of Wight, and it grows two and a half million bulbs a year of 20 different varieties on 60 acres.

Grass

Grass is our most valuable crop because it is the best and cheapest food for the ten million cattle and thirty million sheep in the UK, a country of meat eaters.

Three quarters of all farmland is grass, either permanent pasture or fields known as "leys" which are sown with grass periodically as part of the arable rotation system. The best grassland is on the western side of the UK where rainfall is high and the soils are less suited to arable crops.

Uncultivated grassland on hills, moors, downs and heaths is used for rough grazing but it can only support smaller numbers of animals, mainly sheep, hardy cattle and ponies.

Mowing grass takes place throughout Spring, Summer and Autumn

What it looks like

Grasses have long, narrow leaves and hollow rounded steams. Small flowers are enclosed by a pair of scales – or glumes – and grouped together into spikelets. There are dozens of varieties of grass including Cocksfoot, Timothy and Meadow Fescue. But most of the cultivated grassland grown in the UK is Perennial Rye Grass, which thrives in our climate and is easily digested by sheep and cattle.

The stem apex of the plant (the area of active growth) is protected by new leaves and tillers (shoots). Because it remains at ground level it is not damaged when the grass is grazed or cut. But grass is rarely sown alone on farmland. Agricultural grass mixes sometimes include legumes such as lucerne, trefoil or red or white clover according to the way they will be grazed or the nature of the hay or silage the farmer wishes to cut.

How it is used

Grass is the most important source of food for sheep, cattle and other grazing animals, supplying 70% of their diet. Half of this is grazed in the field, and the rest made into silage or hay for winter feed. The unpredictable British climate makes drying grass for hay a risky business and most cut grass is now turned into silage.

Hay must be dried rapidly, usually in the open, to reduce its moisture content to 15%. By contrast, making silage requires cut grass to be heaped into clamps or collected into bales and the supply of oxygen cut off. In this anaerobic state bacteria in the grass ferments until the material is stable. Moisture content can be 75%.

Did you know ?

- The most common grassland pests are leatherjackets (Daddy Longlegs)
- Wheat, rye, barley and oats are all grasses
- Grass flowers are not always green. Common varieties such as Yorkshire Fog and Marram Grass can appear pink, purple or even white.

Making Hay while, or *if*, the sun shines

For centuries, dried grass or hay has been fed to cattle and other animals over the winter when the farm is too wet for them to graze and the grass in the fields has little nutrient value. If they are allowed to graze when the land is too wet animals will trample or "poach" the ground and make it less productive the following year.

But making hay depends on a prolonged period of dry, sunny weather, otherwise it is too wet to store without mildew forming.

Hay has traditionally been made in midsummer after the grass has flowered and just as it is seeding, but faced with wet summers many farmers are making hay later in the year or whenever the weather forecasters can predict a period of dry, sunny weather.

The grass will be cut and left in swathes or rows. These swathes will be turned two or three times by "tedders" or "swathers" to expose the grass to the air to remove as much moisture as possible. After four or five days, when the moisture content of the hay has been reduced to 15%, it will be baled and taken to barns to store for the winter.

Mown grass drying to make hay

Very often the grass will not dry sufficiently to make good hay. Then farmers will sometimes make big bales of "haylage," a term to describe grass which still has a moisture content of over 50%. It is particularly good for horses.

But most beef and dairy farmers now cut grass when it is shorter and greener and turn it into silage – which is really "pickled" grass stored without oxygen. Silage making is not so dependent on the weather and a farmer can take two or three cuts of silage a year.

The first cut of grass is the most nutritious and plentiful, and is taken around the end of May. As much as ten tons of grass can be cut from one acre. Fertiliser is then added to the cut field and six or eight weeks later a second cut, usually half the amount, is taken. If growing conditions have been good, with enough rain and sun, a grass field may be cut a third time, producing perhaps three tons an acre.

After it is mown, the grass is left to wilt for about 24 hours, turned over to reduce some of the moisture, and then collected in a forage harvester which chops it up and blows it into a trailer. A silage "clamp" or pit is made into which the

Turning hay before baling

Silage bales with attitude

grass is put and spread evenly. A weighted down tractor drives over the top of the clamp to compress the grass and expel the air. The process is repeated with more grass until the pit is full and covered with plastic sheets pulled tight around the edges. The best silage has a moisture content of 75%.

The clamp is weighed down, often with old tyres, until it is needed. Every effort is made to remove trapped air, because this can turn the silage mouldy and make it unusable. When feeding silage to cattle in the winter some farmers add molasses or barley, but good quality silage is an adequate feed by itself.

An alternative method of storing silage is in round bales, wrapped in plastic. This avoids the risk of polluted silage effluent escaping into nearby water supplies, but sealed bales can be punctured by birds and other animals, letting in air and water. This is one reason many farmers are using them less frequently to store their silage. Another is the cost of disposing of the plastic sheets.

Straw

One of the most important agricultural products in the UK is straw – the dried stalks of wheat, barley and oats which are cut when the grain is combined and left in rows in the field. It is normally gathered into large rectangular or round bales, which are heavy to. Small bales can be made for easier delivery.

Straw is used both as a food for cattle and horses, and as winter bedding. Unlike grass, it does not have to be wrapped in plastic or packed in a silage clamp to keep out the oxygen. But while it is baled and often left in an exposed field for a few days, over the winter it must be kept under cover – normally in a barn – to keep it dry and avoid mildew.

Straw lacks the nutrients of hay, and it is not as digestible. But it is a good source of roughage and energy, as long as it is supplemented by compound animal feed. Barley straw is the most nutritious.

From a distance, hay and straw bales can look the same. But hay is heavier than straw and cannot be left outside for any length of time.

Cut straw in the field after combining

Straw bales awaiting collection

Hemp

One of the most versatile crops, hemp can grow almost anywhere and every part of the plant can be used. Because it is part of the cannabis family, it can still only be grown under licence from the Home Office and it is not yet a significant commercial crop in the UK.

Cannabis Sativa
Annual
Grown from: Seed
Harvested: September and October
Rotation: One year in four

Most Prolific Areas of Cultivation:
Limited

What it looks like

Hemp is a member of the hop family, and in warm conditions some varieties can grow to a height of four metres in only 12 weeks. There are many branches on the tall, erect stem and they carry long, serrated, palm-like leaves.

Where you find it

Hemp can grow anywhere but restrictions on its cultivation mean that only licensed growers produce hemp. It is planted in May to avoid frost damage.

How it is used

The value of hemp lies in the oil producing seeds and the stem fibres – much longer, stronger and durable than cotton fibres – which made them ideal for the ropes, sailcloth, sacks, fishing nets and rigging used on ships. In Europe the fibre and shiv (woody core) are a source of biodegradable insulating materials for use in cars and buildings.

Hemp stems are stronger and longer than other cereals

Hemp plants must contain less than 0.02% of the THC chemical which produces narcotic effects, and will be a disappointment to those seeking marijuana and cannabis.

The seeds of the plant are sometimes used in birdseed mixes, which is why cannabis plants sometimes appear unexpectedly near bird feeders. Hemp seed oil, which used to be burned in lamps, is now being cold pressed to produce a cooking and salad oil similar to olive oil but with half the saturated fat and more Omega 3.

Did you know ?

- Because of its strategic importance to shipping, Elizabeth 1st passed a law requiring anyone with arable land to grow a quarter of an acre of hemp
- Jeans were once made of hemp fabric, not cotton, and "denim" is a corruption of "serge de Nimes", which is the French town where the cloth was made
- Hemp fibre is used as a building material in "eco" homes because it is light and offers high levels of insulation

Herbs

There has been a revolution in herb growing in the UK. Polytunnels and glasshouses make it possible to grow a wide range of herbs once only available as imports, and many of them are also grown in miniature versions as intensely-flavoured micro herbs

Grown from:	Seed
Harvested:	May to November
Rotation:	One year in four

Most Prolific Areas of Cultivation:
Herbs are grown throughout the UK, especially in Sussex and the Vale of Evesham

What they look like

Hardier herbs such as lavender, mint or parsley are usually grown in open fields. Others are raised in glasshouses or polytunnels. Most herbs originate from Mediterranean countries and whether they are grown out of doors or under cover they require a well-drained soil and frequent irrigation.

Annuals such as coriander, basil or dill are drilled each year. Perennials such as thyme or sage are planted on average every three years. Most herbs are cut regularly – by hand or machine – over a six or eight week growing cycle. They require warmth and plenty of sunlight, which is why most fresh herbs are not available in the UK after November.

These seasonal constraints do not apply to herbs now being grown in artificial conditions in the new generation of super glasshouses (see Westland Nurseries page 163).

How they are used

British grown herbs are sold fresh (cut or potted) in supermarkets and other retailers and to food processors or caterers to go into prepared meals, sauces (eg pesto or mint sauce) or sandwiches. Some herbs are frozen or dried before sale, and some are grown for medicinal purposes. There is also a growing demand for herb salads in bags.

Some strongly scented herbs such as rosemary and lavender have long been used as the basis of perfumes, soaps and oils, and the medicinal use of herbs has become widespread once more with the growing interest in herbalism.

Did you know ?
- Lavender comes from the Latin word Lavare, to wash
- Israel is the largest supplier of herbs to the UK

Lavender dominates a field with colour and scent

Hops

Fifty years ago hop picking was a productive annual holiday for hundreds of poorer families. Now hops are mainly imported and British growers are struggling to survive.

Hops provide the bitterness in beer, which the British seem to like, despite the complaints of King Henry (see box below). Traditional English "bitter" contains about a third more hops than lager. Thousands of acres across the country, especially in Kent, used to be planted with hops and peppered with the oast houses used to dry the crop.

But while the oast houses remain, largely converted to private homes, the UK market for hops has shrunk dramatically. Increased production in America, Germany and China has led to a collapse in prices, and beer makers are using fewer hops in the brewing process.

What they look like

Hops are climbing plants with a weak stem which have to be supported by poles and

Hops have weak stems and delicate flowers (cones) which must be trained to climb wire frames

Humulus Lupulus	
Perennial	
Grown from:	Seed
Harvested:	September
Average life:	15 years
Most Prolific Areas of Cultivation: Herefordshire, Kent, Sussex and Worcestershire	

wires. In the Spring they are trained to twine around strings attached to the top wire.

Long, thin groups of green flowers called cones form in July. Glands on the flowers give the "hoppy" smell, discourage insects and provide the flavour needed in beer making.

Hop picking, once carried out by dozens of families who moved from the town to the countryside for the labour-intensive work, is now carried out by machine. To aid this process, dwarf hop varieties have been introduced which require a cheaper framework, make spraying easier and allow for better management of soil-borne diseases.

How they are used

Beer making and some flower decoration.

Did you know ?
- Henry the Eighth called hops "A wicked weed that would spoil the taste of the drink and endanger the people"
- A hop field is known as a garden in Kent and a yard in Herefordshire. A new hop garden can cost about £8,000 per acre to build and plant.
- Among the hop varieties grown commercially in the UK are Brewer's Gold, Wye Challenger, Fuggles and Goldings. Varieties for home brewing include 'Prima Donna' and 'Diva'

Kale

Kale is a healthy winter vegetable, but it also provides a "green" source of carbohydrates on which livestock can graze from November to March.

Kale is a very fast-growing and productive crop, yielding up to 30 tons an acre, or six tons for each pound of seed. This productivity, combined with its tolerance of a variety of soil types and weather conditions, has encouraged many dairy farmers to grow kale in place of other forage crops.

Curly Kale for humans....

What it looks like

Most kale is sown in summer to reach maturity in the Autumn. It has long, dark leaves emerging from the top of a thick stem. The most common variety, narrow-stem kale, grows to four feet.

How it is used

Most kale is "strip-grazed" by cattle during the winter. The farmer will put up electric

Brassica oleracea
Annual
Grown from: Seed
Harvested: Autumn and winter
Rotation: One year in four

Most Prolific Areas of Cultivation:
Western regions of the UK

.... and narrow-stem kale for cattle

fences and move them each day to make a new strip of land available for grazing. Cattle and sheep will eat the leaves first and then turn to the nutritious stem. If too much kale is available to the animal at one time, she will eat too much and become bloated.

A Friesian cow can eat one hundredweight (112 lb) of kale a day. When fields are too wet or muddy to graze, a farmer will cut kale and feed it to the cattle separately. Kale can also be made into a silage which is as digestible as grass.

A curly-leafed version of kale is popular as a vegetable for human consumption especially as it is more readily available in the winter, when some other green vegetables are in short supply.

Leek

A popular fresh vegetable throughout the UK, but especially in Wales, where it is a national emblem worn on St David's Day. Home-grown leeks are available most of the year.

Native to the Mediterranean, leeks grow well all over the UK on a wide variety of soils. They can be sown from seed directly into the field or raised in modules under glass and transplanted if they are required to mature early. The lower part is usually blanched by earthing up the stems as the crop grows.

Leeks are hungry vegetables and require plenty of fertiliser. Sandy soil is not suitable for leeks as it becomes trapped between the leaves. Like onions, leeks should not be grown in a field more than one year in five to avoid the spread of the soil-borne disease white rot.

What they look like

Leeks have a white cylindrical stalk rather than the large bulb of their close relative the onion. Above the stalk, wide flat, dark green leaves wrap tightly around each other like a rolled newspaper.

Allium Ameloprasum
Biennial
Grown from: Seed or transplanted
Harvested: Anytime except June
Rotation: One year in five

Most Prolific Areas of Cultivation:
East Anglia, Nottinghamshire, Scotland, Lancashire, Wales, Vale of Evesham

How they are used

Most British leeks sell in shops as fresh vegetables, but a small proportion are used in processed foods, including soups. "Baby" leeks command a higher price.

Did you know ?
- Cock-a-leekie is a Scottish soup made of leeks and chicken broth
- According to legend, Welsh soldiers defeated the Saxons in a field of leeks and wore leeks on their helmets as a symbol of victory
- The Greek physician Hippocrates prescribed the leek as a cure for nose-bleeds

Columns of leeks on the march

Leeks are often bulked up with earth to ensure a white stem

Linseed (Flax)

Once grown for fibre to make clothes, shorter-stemmed varieties of flax are now mainly grown in the UK for their seeds, which are crushed to produce linseed oil. The light blue flowers are a welcome sight in early summer

Linum usitatissimum
Annual
Grown from: Seed
Harvested: August and September
Rotation: One year in four

Most Prolific Areas of Cultivation:
Throughout the UK

Until the Industrial Revolution, most clothes in Europe and America were made of linen, derived from the strong fibres of flax. Nowadays, the plant is grown as a valuable break crop to cereals, and oil is extracted from the seeds.

The cake used after the oil is extracted goes into animal feed. Small quantities of the seeds are used in horse and bird feed.

Linseeds ready to harvest

What it looks like

The distinctive soft blue flowers create a carpet of blue in many parts of Britain in May and June. Flowers have five bright blue petals in a cluster and an unusual characteristic of linseed is the way the petals drop in the early afternoon. At the end of the summer the seed pods turn first light green, then brown, before the crop is combined.

How it is used

Linseed oil is used in the manufacture of paint, linoleum and putty. Unlike varnish, linseed oil soaks into the pores of wood and dries slowly, showing off the grain. Several coats of oil are traditionally used to treat and protect the willow in cricket bats.

Blue linseed flowers in June

Did you know ?

- The words line and linen are both derived from the Latin word linum, meaning flax
- Linseeds are oval and slightly flattened, which makes them difficult to drill and dry evenly.
- Fire Brigades like to treat the wood handles of their metal tools with linseed oil because, unlike synthetic wood finishes, it does not create static electricity

Lucerne

Medicago Sativa

Rich in protein, lucerne is an important animal feed, especially for dairy cattle. It is also known as alfalfa.

Lucerne is similar in appearance to clover, but has deep purple flowers and grows to a height of about three feet. Because it has deep roots, it is resistant to droughts.

Like other legumes, it fixes nitrogen in the soil and has the highest nutritional value of all crops used to make hay because of its high yield per acre and suitablility to make hay or silage on its own without additional grasses.

Lucerne is not normally grazed directly because it can cause bloating in cattle. It is better used for silage or haymaking. It will produce a good crop for at least three years before rotation.

It is also an excellent feed for dairy goats.

Lupins

Lupinus polyphyllus

To most people lupins are an attractive garden or wild flower. Farmers grow them mainly for their seeds, which go into animal feed.

Gardeners grow lupins for their spikes of multicoloured flowers, which may look lovely but are poisonous. Farmers plant a different variety, usually white or blue lupins.

Lupins have a 50% higher protein content than two other legumes, peas and beans. They are also rich in oil. Because of this high nutritional value, most lupins are now grown for their grain, which goes into livestock feed compounds.

The crop is drilled in the spring and combined in the autumn. If they are harvested early, the seeds are moist and can be "crimped" or conditioned, but half will be cut dry. The whole lupin plant can be turned into silage but this is now less common in the UK, and so is the practice of ploughing in the crop as a green manure to enrich the soil.

Maize

It may look like sweetcorn when you drive past it in the field, but in Britain maize is grown to feed cattle, not people. Don't be tempted to pick a cob to eat.

Zea Mays
Annual
Grown from: Seed
Harvested: September and October
Rotation: One year in four

Most Prolific Areas of Cultivation:
Central and Southern England

A ripe corn cob

Maize was grown (and worshipped) by native Americans, and its botanical name "zea mays" means "that which sustains the Mayas". In the UK it mainly sustains cattle and is one of the country's main fodder crops.

What it looks like

The most easily recognisable of all cereal crops because the ear is familiar to most of us as "corn on the cob." Cobs can vary from two inches to two feet in length, with between eight and twenty four rows of kernels. In the UK maize grows to a height of between six and twelve feet, with a cluster of male flowers forming a tassel at the top of the stalk.

Each tassel produces millions of pollen grains which fertilise the female flowers below and cause them to grow into cobs. One maize plant usually has one or two cobs. Traditional corn has round, bulbous kernels, but the most important commercial variety is "dent maize", so called because the soft starch in the middle of the kernels dries more quickly than the surrounding hard starch, leaving dents in the middle.

How it is used

Almost all maize grown in the UK is turned into silage to feed cattle. A separate variety is grown in very small quantities for sweetcorn. Maize starch and syrups are widely used in processed foods and maize flour is used in cakes and biscuits. Maize oil goes into margarine and mayonnaise, and because it can be kept at a high temperature for a long time it is used to fry fish and chips.

Maize for these human uses is mainly imported from the United States, which produces half the world's maize (they call it "corn"). A large proportion of the crop is distilled into ethanol as a fuel for motor vehicles.

Maize for silage

Mangel Wurzels

Beta Vulgaris

Also known as mangolds or mangels, mangel wurzels are the largest root vegetable grown in the UK. They are used mainly as fodder for livestock.

No book on farming can be complete without mention of mangels, even though

their role as a source of additional food for livestock has largely been replaced by fodder beet, which contains more sugar. They are normally left in the field to be strip grazed by cattle, who eat both the root and the leaves.

The large white, yellow or orange yellow roots grow half above and half below soil level. They can be globe or oblong in shape, according to the variety. The deeper root enables the mangel to flourish in the drier parts of south and east England. Above the ground, large dark, glossy leaves extend from prominent yellow stems.

Mangolds are fed to livestock in the winter. They are often cut up before being fed to animals because young livestock would find it difficult to eat a whole mangel root, which can weigh over twenty pounds.

Mustard

Brassica Juncea

Mustard is one of the oldest recorded spices. In the Bible the Kingdom of God is compared to a mustard seed. Nowadays the crop is mainly grown in the UK as a green manure to fertilise the soil. The mustard we buy is made from seeds grown in Canada.

The taste of mustard arises from the sulphur-based essential oils it contains called glucosinolates. Most mustard seed is grown under contract to trading companies who clean, dry, grade, sell and ship it, or in some cases contracted direct to condiment manufacturers likes Colmans of Norwich. It is not home-grown.

Mustard resembles oilseed rape, with which it is sometimes confused. But whereas huge yellow swathes of rape dominate parts of the countryside in April and May, the best time to see the mustard flower, which is not as

yellow as rape, is later in the year. Fully grown plants usually reach about a metre in height.

Mustard grows very quickly, and is often used as a catch crop between two cereals. It is sometimes ploughed back into the fields as a "green manure" or grown so its foliage can provide a cover for game birds on estates used for shooting.

Mushrooms

We produce one third of the mushrooms we eat in the UK, worth about £100 million a year. They are almost all grown in sheds so you can usually smell a mushroom farm before you see it.

Although there are dozens of different mushroom varieties, almost all mushrooms grown commercially in the UK are white agaricus bisporus. The difference in the appearance and size of the mushrooms is due only to the different stage at which they are picked.

What they look like

Button mushrooms double in size every 24 hours to become closed cup, then open cup and finally large flat mushrooms with dark brown gills and flatter caps, similar to wild mushrooms picked in fields. Other edible varieties include brown caps or chestnuts, which have slightly freckled skins, and oyster mushrooms, which come in brown, grey, pink and yellow.

Commercial mushrooms are grown on shelves in pasteurised wheat compost into which spores are added which will "fruit" to become pinhead mushrooms. The compost, with added horse or chicken manure, is kept warm, dark and wet to stimulate ideal growing conditions. When the mushrooms appear – known as a flush – they are handpicked and put in the trays

Did you know ?

- Mushrooms were believed by ancient civilisations to ease the path to immortality. The Romans called them Cibus Deorum or food of the gods
- One mature mushroom can produce 100 million spores
- Mushrooms may lie dormant for many years and only appear when conditions are right

Agaricus Bisporus
Grown from: Spawn
Harvested: Throughout the year

Most Prolific Areas of Cultivation:
Throughout the UK

which will appear on supermarket shelves. The growing cycle lasts between six and eight weeks.

After three flushes the mushroom compost is recycled back to arable farms or garden centres and the growing process begins again on fresh compost.

How they are used

Most mushrooms are sold directly to wholesalers or supermarkets and purchased by shoppers fresh within two or three days. Only 30% of the mushrooms we eat are grown in the UK. The rest come mainly from the Netherlands and Ireland.

Oats

"Oats, a food usually reserved for horses in England, in Scotland supports the people," said Samuel Johnson. But the amount of oats grown in the UK, whether for horses or people, has been falling for several years.

Avena Sativa	
Annual	
Grown from:	Seed
Harvested:	July and August
Rotation:	One year in four

Most Prolific Areas of Cultivation:
Scotland and North of England

Oats are a much more hardy cereal than wheat and require less sun. They will grow in cool, moist climates and poor soil. They have slowly been replaced in many areas by barley, which is easier to harvest and has higher yields. Oats are a valuable break crop in cereal rotation because they have no genetic connection to wheat or barley, and don't share the same diseases.

What the crop looks like

Easily distinguishable from wheat and barley by the way the grain spreads outwards from the stem and the ears hang down. Whole oat grains are known as groats. Long and thin, they look similar to brown rice.

How it is used

Oats are used mainly for animal feed, being fed to horses, cattle and dogs. Oat straw, which is soft, absorbent and relatively dust-free, is used as bedding for horses and cattle.

But oats have specialist human uses, too, especially in Scotland and the north of England. Pinhead oats (grains chopped into two or three pieces) and oatmeal make the best porridge. Rolled or flattened oats can be eaten raw in muesli or granola, and used to make biscuits or flapjacks.

Whole oats contain more fibre than other grains which is why they are considered an important ingredient of a healthy diet.

Did you know ?
- An oat bath is thought to relieve skin conditions, and oats are used in many cosmetics

A field of oats in early summer........and at harvest time

Oilseed Rape

Rape has become a financial lifeline for many farmers, blanketing fields with a rich yellow canopy when it flowers in April and May. It is also an important "break" crop for many farmers.

Brassica Napus	
Annual	
Grown from:	Seed
Harvested:	August and September
Rotation:	One year in five
Most Prolific Areas of Cultivation: Throughout the UK	

A field of rape lights up the landscape

Rape, which seems to be grown more widely every year, has become a vital crop for British farmers because of its high oil and protein content. It is the third most important arable crop in the UK (after wheat and barley) Rape is rotated with cereals because it improves the soil and "breaks" the cycle of cereal diseases and pests.

What it looks like

Rape grows to a height of 1.5 metres and the brassy yellow (sticky) flowers smell slightly of honey. The leaves on the main stalk resemble dandelion leaves and

because both plants flower in April it is possible from a distance to confuse a field of rape with a field of dandelions. The seed pods, which are pointed at both ends and extend from the stems below the flowers, contain tiny round black seeds like ballbearings.

How it is used

The seeds are crushed to extract oil which goes into a wide range of products to feed humans and animals. The residue – a high protein "meal" – is mainly used in animal feedstuffs. A non-edible variant of rapeseed oil is used for a variety of industrial purposes, including biofuels. The oil is high in monounsaturates and because it is odourless it is widely used as a cooking oil and an ingredient in "healthy" food products. It is also used in the manufacture of margarine, crisps, mayonnaise and ice cream.

Did you know ?
- Slugs and pigeons can destroy whole fields of rape
- The tiny round rapeseeds are dangerous to walk on because they flow like water
- Hay fever sufferers blame pollen from rape for making their condition worse, but allergy to rape pollen is rare

below left: *Rape flowers in April*
right: *Rape ready for harvest in August*

Onion

An edible bulb believed to originate from South West Asia, the onion is eaten across the world by more people than any other vegetable.

The onion is part of the lily family, like chives, spring onions, garlic, leeks and shallots. Common bulb onion varieties include the red, the brown, the large Spanish, and the white onion. Pearl onions are small white onions used for pickling.

What they look like

Onions, which are biennial, have a cluster of small, greenish white flowers on one or more leafless stalks in their second year. They may be grown from seed or from sets which are started from seed the previous year. As they prefer warm, sunny conditions, most onions are grown in the east of England.

They can be planted in early to mid Spring. Some varieties can be planted in the autumn and harvested earlier. Bulbs are ready to harvest when the stalks drop. These tops are removed before the onions are lifted by machinery which undercuts the crop. Most onions are dried in temperature controlled storehouses, and warm air completes the drying process to produce the golden brown colour of onion skins. Stores can be refrigerated to 1°C over winter to extend availability.

Did you know ?
- Onions are believed to absorb impurities from the air and thus prevent or cure fevers or colds
- Slicing onions causes tears because they contain an oil rich in sulphur. Small droplets irritate the nerve endings in the eye where they form an acid.
- Nobody seems to know the true origin of the phrase "Know your onions"!

Allium cepa
Biennial
Grown from: Seed or sets
Harvested: July to September
Rotation: One year in six

Most Prolific Areas of Cultivation:
Eastern England

How they are used

Most onions are sold as fresh vegetables but a sizeable quantity go to the catering industry and manufacturers peeled, diced or as onion rings. Some go into other food products such as onion powder (ground dehydrated onion), onion salt (onion powder and salt), onion flakes and flavouring cubes. Onions are also sold canned or pickled (usually pearl onions) and frozen (whole or chopped).

Young onions

Parsnip

Pastinaca Sativa

About three thousand hectares of farmland across the UK are planted with parsnips, the same acreage as brussels sprouts. They are harvested throughout the winter.

Parsnips need frost to develop their full flavour and are not suitable for warmer climates. Like the carrot, its close relative, the parsnip can be bulbous or long and

tapered. The name parsnip derives from a Latin word for "forked."

Supermarkets like clean, "white" straight roots without the "fangs" that sometimes develop at the end of the parsnip, and this regular shape is best achieved by planting in deep sandy soils without stones.

While they still have their green tops, parsnips can be harvested by "top" lifters, which pull them from the ground. Later they need machines which will dig them out like potatoes.

Parsnips can be boiled, roasted or made into soups and casseroles. They can also be fried or eaten raw. In mediaeval times, before sugar was used, parsnips were sometimes used to sweeten stews and other dishes.

Pears

Pyrus Communis

The number of pear orchards in the UK, mainly in Herefordshire and Kent, is dwarfed by the acreage of apple trees.

Some growers have grubbed up their pear orchards in favour of more productive apples, but the growing popularity of cider has extended to pear cider or perry and this has given some boost to demand.

Pears come into blossom earlier than apples and while they are less able to withstand drought, they can cope with colder temperatures. Many English orchards consist of older, less productive trees which are being replaced. New orchards are being planted with the trees closer together and they are pruned much harder to achieve greater yields. The new generation of pear trees are able to produce fruit in their second year.

The most popular varieties remain Conference, Comice and Concorde. Most pears are purchased as fresh fruit in season, with a small quantity going to make perry (pear cider).

Peas

Peas remain one of our most popular table vegetables, especially among children, even if few people now eat peas fresh from the pod. Over half the pea crop in the UK is frozen. Most of the rest goes into animal feed.

Fresh peas are harvested from the vine by a specialist harvester that is able to remove the pea without damage, which is why they are known as vining peas. They are mainly grown in East Anglia and South East Scotland and frozen within minutes for major supermarket suppliers.

The rest of the UK pea crop ("field" or "combinable" peas) are harvested with a combine harvester, usually in August. These peas are cut when they are dry and are stored like any other cereals, mainly for animal feed. Some dairy farmers include field peas in silage. One of the biggest problem with field peas is "lodging" - their tendency to fall over when they are mature, which makes combining more difficult.

Like other legumes, such as beans or lupins, peas add nitrogen to the soil and are a valuable break crop to allow fields to recover after cereals in a rotation system. Wheat is often planted after peas because it benefits most from the improved soil fertility.

What they look like

Field peas are grown without artificial support, with long, light-green tendrils and mainly white flowers in May. Pods appear in June.

How they are used

Over half the UK pea crop – that proportion which is harvested when the peas are dried out - is used as animal feed, either milled by farmers themselves or turned into compounds by animal feed suppliers. Some are canned, used in pet food mixes, or turned into processed or mushy peas. Green peas are almost all frozen for human consumption.

Pisum Sativum
Annual
Grown from: Seed
Harvested: June to September
Rotation: One year in six

Most Prolific Areas of Cultivation:
East Anglia, South East Scotland

Did you know ?

- The popularity of frozen peas owes much to Clarence Birdsye, the scientist who discovered the best method of preserving and freezing food
- Peas are self-pollinating and do not rely on bees and other insects
- Black Eyed Peas are a variety of bean, not pea

Peppers and Chillies

Chillies come in all sizes, shapes and colours

Capsicum Annuum	
Annual	
Grown from:	Seed
Harvested:	July to November

The popularity of peppers or capsicums has changed the appearance of the supermarket vegetable counter. The development of huge, heated greenhouses has made it possible to grow them in the UK and reduce our reliance on imported peppers.

Chillies and peppers contain the chemical capsaicin, which causes the body to sweat and the pulse to quicken. As blander Western diets have given way to spicier foods, our tolerance of capsaicin has risen, leading to more ambitious (and hotter) chilli dishes.

What they look like

Most peppers are bell shaped, but chillies – the seed pods of the capsicum plant - come in all shapes, sizes and colours. They may be long and thin, or almost tomato like in appearance, and may be picked while still green or with richer red, yellow, orange and purple colours later in the season. Varieties grown in England include the Jalapeno, the Whippet's Tail, the Hungarian Hot Wax, the Habenero and the Spanish Fryer.

Where you find them

Peppers are grown under glass or in polytunnels by specialist growers in the south and east of England. Specialist chilli growers can be found as far apart as Cornwall and Northumberland. One of the largest is the South Devon Chilli farm near Kingsbridge, which grows 100 different varieties and harvests between three and six tons a year.

How they are used

Peppers are roasted, stir fried and added to salads. Chillies are used in a range of processed foods including curries. They are also used to make pickles, sauces or even chocolate. Capsaicin can disable part of the nervous system and is an important ingredient in painkilling drugs.

Did you know ?

- The world's best-selling chilli condiment is Tabasco sauce
- Humans are the only mammals to eat chillies
- One of the world's hottest chillies is the Dorset Naga, developed from a Bangladeshi strain on a chilli farm near Dorchester

Most peppers in the UK are grown under cover

Phacelia

Phacelia Tanacetifolia

Phacelia is grown on farmland as a green manure to plough back into the soil, usually on field margins.

Phacelia is a green manure

A native of North America, phacelia can be planted at any time in the summer and is fully grown in two months. It can be between six inches and four feet in height with ferny foliage and attractive clusters of blue or mauve flowers.

These continue for six weeks and attract large numbers of bees and other pollinating insects, which is why phacelia is popular in the Government scheme under which farmers are encouraged to leave unimproved grassland on the edges of fields to encourage wildlife.

English names for phacelia include fiddleneck, lacy scorpion-weed, wild heliotrope, and bee's friend. As well as increasing soil fertility, phacelia helps to prevent leaching and soil erosion which might otherwise occur if land is left unplanted.

Plums

Prunus Domestica

Most of the plums we buy in shops are imported, and less than a thousand hectares are grown commercially in the UK. But home grown plums are available from July until September.

The biggest sellers are Victoria plums, which are picked in August. Early varieties include Opals, Avalon and Jubilee, while Marjorie Seedlings are picked later. One of the best known plums is the Pershore Yellow Egg, usually grown for making jam.

Plums are most commonly found in Kent and the Value of Evesham. Like apples, new plum plants are grafted on to the rootstock of older trees.

Greengages and damsons flower in the same period and may cross-pollinate with plums.

Plum blossom and fruit is now a rare sight in the UK

Potatoes

Over a hundred thousand hectares of potatoes are grown in the UK and they are our most important vegetable. Because they can grow in wet and cold conditions they are found throughout the country.

It is thought that potatoes originate from the slopes around Lake Titicaca in Peru, where native Indians first realised the potential of the "batata" – as they called it – and began to cultivate it. Spanish soldiers brought potatoes to Europe and, if tales are to be believed, Sir Walter Raleigh also brought them back from North America.

What they look like

Potatoes need regular spraying to prevent disease

The potato plant grows to between one and three feet high. Large dark green leaves on several stems are topped by small white, yellow or purple flowers. The swellings or tubers on the underground shoots of the plant form the potatoes and the "eyes" on the tuber, which sometimes disfigure the potato, are leaf buds.

Prone to potato blight and other diseases, the vegetable must be sprayed regularly to keep it disease-free.

Common varieties are Charlotte (for salads), King Edwards, Desiree, Romano and Maris Piper. New potatoes, which attract a much higher price than "main crop" potatoes, are harvested in early summer in frost-free areas such as West Cornwall and Pembrokeshire.

Solanum tuberosum	
Annual	
Grown from:	Tuber
Harvested:	April (new potatoes) to November
Rotation:	One year in four
Most Prolific Areas of Cultivation: Throughout the UK	

Did you know ?

- To persuade people that potatoes were good for humans as well as animals to eat a French scientist called Parmentier put a guard on his potato field. His neighbours assumed they were valuable and started to eat them
- Exposure to light turns a potato green
- The Irish potato famine in the 1840s led to the death of over a million people

How they are used

Farmers used to grow potatoes mainly as animal food and for many years they were considered fit only for poor people to eat. Now they are grown mainly for human consumption although we now buy as much processed potato (crisps and frozen chips and waffles etc) as we do the fresh vegetable.

Newly-sown potatoes are "earthed up" in ridges

Runner Beans

Phaseolus caccineus

Runner beans are one of our most popular garden or allotment vegetables, and they are also a commercially important crop in several parts of the UK.

Commercially-grown runner beans are raised in the same way as those grown at home, climbing on frames, wires and bamboo sticks. An earlier crop is grown under fleece or plastic covers for picking in June, but most runners are grown in the open. They are picked by hand for the fresh market.

Dwarf or French beans (phaseolus vulgaris) have a similar season, are grown from seed and also hand-picked for the fresh market. They are free-standing and grow to a height of 12 – 18 inches. A small quantity are machine harvested for freezing.

Broad beans (vicia faba) are harvested before they are fully mature, while they are still light green. The pods are hand-picked if the beans are going to be sold fresh, but when they are grown for freezing a large vining machine, similar to that used for harvesting peas, is used.

Rhubarb

Rheum rhabarbarum

Traditionally grown in the "rhubarb triangle" of West Yorkshire, rhubarb is technically a vegetable and not a fruit. It is gaining popularity as a so-called "super food".

The cold and wet climate of the UK suits rhubarb, but the season is short and in winter the leaves die down and the rhubarb shoots or stalks only emerge in the Spring. To extend the season, much British rhubarb is now "forced," being grown in dark sheds heated to 60 degrees and cut between January and April.

It originates in Siberia, but the similarities in climate are not the reason the area between Bradford, Wakefield and Leeds became known as the Rhubarb Triangle. The local textile industry produced "shoddy" – the knots and other wastes from the combing process. The shoddy, mixed with horse manure and other organic matter is applied as a top dressing and breaks down to supply nitrogen to the rhubarb roots.

The only edible part of the rhubarb, the celery-like leafstalks, grow up to two feet tall. Those grown out of doors tend to be redder than those grown under cover.

Rye

The hardiest of the cereals, rye is sown in soils which are too poor to produce a good crop of wheat. Together with Triticale (see below) it represents less than one percent of cereals grown in the UK.

What it looks like

Rye is more likely to be confused with barley than wheat. The ears have whiskers (awns) and reach about a metre above the ground.

How it is used

Rye grain goes into livestock feed and silage, and some is used to make flour for rye bread, pumpernickel and crisp bread. Rye beer and whiskey use a small proportion of the UK's production. Rye bread (traditionally dark brown in colour) is usually made with sourdough rather than yeast.

When not harvested, it is useful as a cover crop or green manure to improve soil, especially clay, because it has extensive roots. Although rye can be grazed it can give a distinct taste to the milk of dairy cows.

Triticale

A hybrid of rye and durum wheat which has been "man-made" to combine the hardiness of rye and the yield of wheat. The name comes from the Latin terms for wheat (triticum) and rye (secale). It is widely used in livestock feed, particularly for pigs and poultry. Triticale is drilled in September and October and harvested in August.

Newer Spring varieties are being planted in livestock areas on the west of the UK, including Northern Ireland, often with peas and lupins, and used as forage for animals to eat in the field.

Secale Cereale
Annual or Perennial
Grown from: Seed
Harvested: August
Rotation: One year in four

Most Prolific Areas of Cultivation:
Acid soils in the east of the UK

Rye

Did you know ?
- A fungus called ergot frequently grows on rye and humans who consume ergot-infected rye may contract a serious medical condition called ergotism which can cause convulsions and miscarriages

Triticale

Salads

Once upon a time we used to eat lettuce. Now we are just as likely to buy bagged salad leaves, which has introduced us to a range of leafy salads not widely eaten or grown in the country before

Grown from: Seed/Seedling
Harvested: May to October

Most Prolific Areas of Cultivation:
East Anglia, South Coast of England, West Midlands, Evesham, Lancashire

Salads grow well in the temperate climate of the UK, as leafy salads grow best in an even temperature. Growing them outdoors makes for strong and healthy plants. Mesh nets are used to keep out pests such as aphids. In summer more than ninety per cent of the salads we eat are grown in the UK.

Some growers produce fresh lettuces throughout the year in glasshouses and polytunnels, either in soil mulched with polythene to control weeds or using a hydroponic system in which the lettuce is grown in troughs filled with liquid nutrients.

What it looks like
Salads are made either of "wholehead" lettuces such as cos, or plants which are grown for their individual leaves, like rocket. These can be harvested by machine, but wholehead lettuces must be picked by hand to avoid damage.

Common lettuces in the UK are iceberg, gem, cos, butterheads and oak leaf. Leaves grown for salads include spinach, rocket, watercress, red chard, curly endive (frisée) and lambs lettuce or mache.

How it is used
Lettuces and salad leaves are sold fresh for salads, garnishes and making into soups. Half British salad production is sold as individual lettuces, the rest in bagged or prepared salads. Salad leaves are kept cool after picking and transported to wholesalers and retailers in refrigerated vehicles to maintain freshness.

Did you know ?
• Romaine lettuces have become known as cos because they are thought to have originated in the Greek island of Kos

Salads grow well outdoors in the UK's temperate climate

Soft Fruit

Most of the soft fruit grown commercially in the UK is raised under cover to protect it from the vagaries of the British climate. The strawberry crop alone is worth £200 million pounds a year.

The most popular soft fruit in Britain is the strawberry. Not just with cream, and not just in Wimbledon Week. Followed by raspberries, blackcurrants, blueberries, gooseberries and blackberries. As the growing season has extended, sales of soft fruit in the UK have doubled and the proportion that are home grown has risen.

Most berries are grown under cover, usually in polytunnels which protect them from rain and wind and ensure the berries can be picked for a six month season from May until October. Some berries are grown out of doors in growbags. Sales of home-grown blueberries have increased substantially in recent years.

Most soft fruit is picked by hand although automated picking is common for some berries such as blackcurrants. Finding labour to pick the fruit is one of the biggest challengers for soft fruit growers, and when harvests are plentiful some fruit can be lost because there are not enough people to pick it. Most fruit pickers in the UK are seasonal workers from Eastern Europe.

How they are used

In season, most strawberries and raspberries are sold fresh in supermarkets, greengrocers and farm shops. Eighty per cent of the home-grown strawberries available in UK supermarkets are the Elsanta variety. Many farms invite the public to pick their own soft fruit. But a large quantity goes into yoghurts, ice cream, sorbets, cordials, juices and processed tarts and puddings. There is a growing demand for frozen fruit and mixed berries.

Did you know ?
- 90% of the UK blackcurrant production goes into blackcurrant juice
- Spectators at Wimbledon eat over 60,000 pounds of strawberries each year
- "Gooseberry" was once another word for the Devil, and may explain why "playing gooseberry" is so unwelcome

Gooseberry   *Raspberry*

Spinach

Spinacea Oleracea

Spinach is a rich source of vitamins, folic acid and minerals, especially iron. The leaves shrink dramatically when they are cooked, and so does the value of the nutrients they contain.

Baby leaf spinach is the most common variety grown in Britain, and is normally sold in salad packs. Larger spinach leaves are a separate variety best cooked.

Spinach is planted as a seed in spring and is grown out of doors, mainly in the southern half of the United Kingdom. It is at its best from May to October, but is now available all year round with imports providing winter supplies. The UK grows 60% of the spinach it consumes.

Chard, or Swiss Chard, is sometimes known as perpetual spinach and it is also used both in salads and cooked. But it comes from the beetroot family and has shiny, green, ribbed leaves, with stems that vary in colour from white to yellow to red.

Catherine de Medici, who came from Florence, is supposed to have liked spinach so much that she had it served at every meal, which is why dishes made with spinach are known as "Florentine."

Swede

Brassica Napus

The Scots know them as neeps, an essential component of a Burns Night supper, but they are equally important as a feedstuff for sheep and cattle.

Believed to have originated from Scandinavia, the swede was an important food in Northern Europe before the introduction of potatoes. In the UK they are grown in wetter parts of the country, particularly Devon and North East Scotland.

Sometimes known as the Swedish turnip or yellow turnip, the swede is known in many countries as the rutabaga, from the Swedish for "root ram."

Long, smooth, thin leaves emerge from a dull yellow root, which has a distinct "neck," tinged purple, green or bronze. One third, or less, of the root lies above the ground.

Most of us eat them as a winter vegetable, usually mashed. They are an even more important feedstuff for sheep and cattle, being eaten in the field or clamped and stored for winter.

Sugar Beet

Sugar Beet is one of the country's most important arable crops, providing half of our sugar. A hybrid version is grown as fodder beet, a valuable winter feed for livestock.

The British climate is too wet and cold to grow sugar cane, but it is ideal for sugar beet. The first sugar beet factory was opened in Norfolk in 1912 but the industry really expanded in the Second World War, when imports of sugar cane from the West Indies were restricted and the Government encouraged farmers to grow sugar beet for home consumption.

What it looks like

Sugar beet is planted in rows about 50 cms apart. Above the ground a larger, shinier, heart-shaped leaf distinguishes sugar beet from other root crops such as swede or turnip. Below the ground, the beet is not unlike a large parsnip in appearance. It is cut by forage harvesters, which cut off the green leaves and lift the roots out of the ground.

How it is used

Because it is heavy and bulky to transport, almost all sugar beet is processed close to where it is grown in the large factories owned by the giant British Sugar company in East Anglia and the East Midlands.

Beta Vulgaris	
Biennial	
Grown from:	Seed
Harvested:	September to March
Rotation:	One year in four
Most Prolific Areas of Cultivation:	
East Angia and East Midlands	

The newly-cleaned beet is sliced into strips which are put into boiling water. This sugar solution is then concentrated by evaporating and boiling and "seeded" with fine grounds of sugar, which grow into crystals. Spinning in a centrifuge separates the sugar from the syrup and the white crystals are dried and stored in silos. The syrup that remains after two further crystallisations is called molasses and is used in animal feed.

Did you know ?
- The harvesting period for sugar beet is known by farmers as the "campaign." It takes place between September and March when the level of sugar in the beet is highest

A different variety of beet – fodder beet - is an important winter food for cattle. It can be stored in clamps for several months and has largely replaced the mangel-wurzel.

Sugar Beet makes sugar

Fodder Beet feeds animals

Sunflower

Sunflowers have been grown as a farm crop in southern England since the Second World War but late harvests and low yields mean that only about 500 hectares are planted each year.

The sunflower gets its name from the Greek words helios meaning sun and anthos meaning flower. Sunflowers are easy to grow provided they have direct sun. They will tolerate a wide range of soils and require little nitrogen. But they cannot be planted until April or May when the soil is relatively warm.

What they look like

Large flower heads with big dark brown centres and bright yellow petals. New varieties may have orange or maroon petals. Semi-dwarf varieties which mature early are best suited to the English climate.

How they are used

Almost all the sunflower crop grown commercially in the UK is either used to provide bird seed or goes into pet food. Sunflower seeds are high in energy and provide many of the nutrients that most wild birds need. The seed makes excellent chicken-food and feeding hens on bruised sunflower seeds is known to increase their laying power.

There is a big market for sunflower oil to use in cooking and salads because it is high in polyunsaturated fats, but almost all the oil currently used in the UK is imported. Sunflower seed snacks are increasingly popular and sunflower oil is sometimes used as a biofuel.

Did you know ?

- In Peru, the Aztecs worshiped sunflowers and crowned their kings in the bright yellow flowers
- The sunflower follows the movement of the sun from east in the morning to west in the afternoon. Once the flower opens, most sunflowers face east
- Sunflower pollen stains when dropped, which is why pollenless varieties have been developed

Tomatoes

To meet our huge appetite for tomatoes giant glasshouses are being built all over England. But we still produce only a fifth of the tomatoes we eat.

Lycopersicon esculentum
Annual
Grown from: Seed
Harvested: February to November

Most Prolific Areas of Cultivation:
England

Almost all British tomatoes are grown in glasshouses, and there are over 500 acres of these across the country. We produce twenty percent of the tomatoes we consume, the rest coming mainly from Spain, Holland and the Canary Islands.

Tomatoes are easily damaged by wind or extremes of temperature. Growing them in heated glasshouses means British tomatoes are available from March to November and growers can introduce predators such as wasps to control pests.

Some tomato glasshouses have combined heat and power plants sited nearby. Hot water from the CHP plant, which would be wasted through cooling towers in normal power generation, then provides heat for the tomatoes, Carbon dioxide from the CHP plants is also pumped into the glasshouses to aid photosynthesis.

What they look like

Peat is no longer used to grow tomatoes commercially. They are raised in an artificial substance known as rockwool, to which water and other nutrients are added, or grow in recycled material such as coir or wood fibre. Although tomatoes "self pollinate" the process is aided by bumblebees, which help the stamens to shed their pollen. The yellow flowers turn into ripe tomatoes in 40 – 60 days.

Traditional "round" tomatoes make up half the British crop, but cherry, cocktail, plum and beef tomatoes are also grown. Half the crop is cut and sold "on the vine," which allows them to be picked when they are fully ripe.

How they are used

Almost all tomatoes grown in the UK are bought fresh. Canned tomatoes, tomato ketchup and tomato juice are made from imported tomatoes.

Tomatoes in the UK are increasingly sold on the vine

Did you know ?

- Tomatoes – or tomati – were first grown by the Incas and Aztecs
- The first cultivated tomatoes were yellow (golden apples or pommes d'or in French). They are still known as pomodoro in Italian

Turnip

Brassica Campestris

We know them as a tasty root vegetable to accompany roasts and stews but "stubble turnips" are one of the most important fodder crops for livestock, especially sheep,

The humble turnip has a unique place in British agriculture. Introduced from Eastern Europe in the 16th century, it enabled farmers to feed cattle and sheep over the winter instead of slaughtering them in the Autumn when the grass stopped growing.

Lord Townshend, a Norfolk landowner, showed how root crops could feed livestock in the winter. "Turnip Townshend" also showed the benefits of growing the crop in rotation to avoid having to leave a field fallow for a year.

Turnips, like other root crops, "clean" the soil and prevent the growth of weeds.

The turnip is very similar to the swede, with a white root and a spray of mid-green flattish leaves. Half the root grows above ground and turns purple when exposed to the sunlight. Unlike swede, the leaves emerge directly from the top of the root, without a "neck."

Sheep and cattle can eat turnip tops in the field in autumn and the roots can be stored to provide food for the winter. Some turnips grown as forage are known as "stubble turnips" because they are sown into the stubble of cereal crops at the end of summer.

Watercress

Rorippanasturtium aquaticum

As its name suggests, watercress grows in water rather than soil. The crop, worth over fifty million pounds a year, is almost all grown on the chalk downs of Dorset and Hampshire.

Watercress is grown in shallow gravel beds fed by springs and bore-holes providing a constant flow of chalk filtered spring water.

The growing time can then be anything from 28 to 70 days, depending on the weather. The warmer it is the faster the plants grow.

When the watercress is ready for harvesting, highly specialised harvesting machines cut up to two to three tonnes of watercress an hour.

One or two specialist herb and salad producers have started to grow watercress in soil and a consortium of traditional growers have sought European authority to make it illegal for them to sell this as watercress.

Harvesting watercress

Wheat

This is where our daily bread comes from – and our pasta, porridge, biscuits and breakfast cereals. It is the most important arable crop in the UK, worth over twenty billion pounds a year.

> ### *Triticum*
> Annual
> Grown from: Seed
> Harvested: July and August
> Rotation: One year in four
>
> **Most Prolific Areas of Cultivation:**
> **Eastern England and Scotland**

Wheat is the most widely grown arable crop in the UK covering nearly two million hectares. Like other cereal crops, it is a cultivated grass which originates from the Middle East. Most wheat in the UK is planted in the autumn ("winter wheat") and harvested in August.

What it looks like

The two most common species of wheat are aestivum (for bread) and durum (for pasta), although this is less common in the UK. They both grow to about a metre in height and the ears remain upright until harvest. Modern wheat has evolved through cross breeding of traditional varieties such as einkorn, emmer and spelt.

> ### Did you know ?
> • Gluten, a protein found in wheat, cannot be tolerated by one per cent of the population who have celiac disease
> • Most breads are made with wheat flour, including those like rye and oat breads which are named after the other grains they contain
> • Britain is a major exporter of wheat

The development of shorter stemmed dwarf wheat – which is less likely to be flattened by strong winds - has led to a huge increase in grain production across the world. Taller wheat varieties, such as Hunstman, are still grown for their thatching straw.

How it is used

Wheat grain is used to feed humans and animals. Grain for flour attracts a higher price and goes into the baking of bread, biscuits, cakes, pasta and a wide range of other foods. Lower quality grain goes into cattle and poultry feed and some is used to make bioethanol. Starch and sugar from wheat is used in confectionery, soft drinks, alcoholic drinks and convenience foods. Wheat straw is used for animal feed, bedding, thatch and as a biofuel.

The ears of wheat remain upright until harvest

Willow

Willow is harvested every three years

Salix
Perennial
Grown from: Rods or cuttings

Most Prolific Areas of Cultivation:
Throughout the UK

You can make baskets, fences, coffins and cricket bats from willow, but much of the fast-growing crop is now being burnt in power stations to generate "green" electricity.

Willow is a broadleaved hardwood tree which has traditionally been grown to provide hurdles for fences or basket making, with one specialist variety grown to make cricket bats. But willow is now being coppiced on a large scale as a biomass energy crop.

What it looks like

Willow trees are often found near rivers and streams. They have tall stems and light, flowery foliage. They are planted in rows well apart to allow plenty of light. When coppiced, shoots will grow two metres in a year and when they are harvested every three years they can be six metres tall.

Before planting, manure or sewage sludge is often applied to retain moisture in the ground and increase yields. The crop will be cut back close to the ground during the first winter after planting to encourage coppicing. Fencing may be needed to discourage rabbits and deer from eating the new shoots.

How it is used

One hectare of short rotation coppice willow will produce ten tons of woodchips a year which can generate one kilowatt of electricity when burnt in a power station. Willow grown in this way can be harvested every three years and a plantation will be viable for 25 to 30 years before it has to replaced.

Willow is "carbon neutral" which means the amount of carbon dioxide released in the burning of the willow pellets is equivalent to the amount absorbed by the willow as it grows. Emissions caused by transporting the pellets is reduced when the crop is burnt in local power stations or used in boilers heating homes and offices close to the plantation.

The specialist growth of cricket bat willows is mainly carried out in Sussex and Kent. A number of willow growers, many of them located on the Somerset Levels, are supplying ready-made baskets, garden furniture and coffins woven from willow cane.

Did you know ?
- The Weeping Willow is an ornamental tree which is not coppiced
- Poplar, ash, birch and hazel are among other trees suitable for burning as biomass

Wine

The quality of wine produced in England and Wales has improved in recent years and if global warming raises temperatures, some believe the limestone and chalk escarpments of South East England may one day offer serious competition to French producers.

There have been vineyards in England since the time of the Norman Conquest, many of them in monasteries. The Domesday Book records them in 46 different places in the south of England. Winemaking almost died out after Tudor times, and this may have been because of changes in the climate or the dissolution of the monasteries.

Perennial	
Grown from:	Vines grafted onto rootstock
Harvested:	September and October
Most Prolific Areas of Cultivation: Southern England and Wales	

It can be four years before the first crop is ready to pick. All the foliage dies away after harvest, and over the winter vines are cut back hard and trained along wires or trellises to a height of three or four feet. New growth appears in the spring but a hard frost during the flowering can destroy a year's crop. Vines continue to yield commercial quantities of grapes for up to 30 years.

How it is used

Sparkling white wine is the most popular wine from English and Welsh vineyards, and is produced in the champagne style – fermented in the bottle. Large quantities of still white wine are also produced, and rose is becoming more popular. Only ten per cent of domestic wine production is red.

Did you know ?
- "British Wine" is the term used to describe wine made in the UK from imported grapes or grape juice
- In the reign of Henry the Second, wine in England cost a penny a gallon
- Only one per cent of the wine we drink is from UK vineyards

Vines are cut back hard each year

It has resumed again since the Second World War and in an average year about two million bottles of wine are produced from UK vineyards.

What it looks like

Most of the grapes grown on the 400 plus British vineyards are used to make white wine or champagne, although the grapes themselves may be red or white. White varieties include Reichensteiner, Bacchus, Seyval Blanc and Chardonnay. Reds include Pinot Noir and Dornfelder.

To Plough or Not to Plough?
Preparing the land for new crops

Traditionally the cropping cycle on a farm begins when fields are ploughed in the autumn or spring to bury the harvest "trash" (the stubble and other remains of the previous crop) and turn the soil to expose it to the air.

But while most farmers in Britain continue to plough, and take great pride in creating evenly spaced and cut furrows of shiny black, brown or – in the case of South Devon – red soil, an increasing number have stopped.

There are two reasons for the decline of ploughing. One is cost. It takes time and skill to plough a field, and this means many hours in the tractor. At a time when farm incomes have declined dramatically the costs of ploughing, often in difficult, damp conditions, cannot always be justified. And ploughed land still has to be harrowed and rolled before crops can be sown.

The other is effectiveness. A new generation of cultivators which can prepare a seedbed without turning over the soil can travel much more quickly, and they incorporate the harrowing and rolling function. Some of them also incorporate a seed drill.

This process is called either direct drilling or minimum tillage ("mintil" to many farmers)

and has environmental benefits because there is less disruption to the soil. More worms survive and there is often less standing water in the fields. The disadvantage is that grass and other unwanted seeds may germinate more easily.

Minimum tillage is becoming increasingly popular in fields where cereals are grown. Where necessary, these will be sprayed with pesticides beforehand to kill off excess weeds.

Nutrients removed from the soil have to be replaced, either with animal or human manure, compost or chemical fertilisers, if its fertility is to be maintained. Decomposing plant material, or humus, is ploughed back into the soil to raise fertility. Where cattle are kept, their waste is stored and returned to the fields over the winter as slurry or solid manure.

But on farms that don't keep livestock – pure cereal, vegetable or fruit growers – animal waste is normally not available in the quantities required and the most important nutrients needed by growing plants – nitrogen, potassium and phosphorous – are normally provided by fertilisers. The soil will be measured regulary to check the presence of these nutrients.

A conventionally ploughed field

Land that has been ripped for direct drilling

Some plants, such as peas and beans, return nitrogen to the soil naturally. They are known as legumes, a family of plants that are able to make use of atmospheric nitrogen to enrich the protein content of both the plant and seed. Legumes do this by utilising bacteria that inhabit nodules in the roots that "fix" the nitrogen, which becomes available to the following crop.

When a large number of plants of the same type are grown together in a field, weeds, pests and diseases spread more quickly. If the same crop is grown for several years, the weeds become stronger and crop yields reduce. This is why crop rotation is so important. Planting a different crop breaks this cycle.

"Break" crops like sugar beet have different characteristics to cereals such as wheat or barley and are not affected by the same pests and diseases. But even when crops are rotated effectively, most farmers still need to use weedkillers (herbicides) and pesticides on a regular basis to ensure good yields.

Lime is often spread before crops are planted to combat acidity in the soil. The acid/alkali balance of the soil must be measured, and normally lime will be spread on a prepared field to be harrowed and rolled into the ground.

Spreading lime on newly cultivated field

Dung Heaps ready to spread

Both of these processes must take place well before the new crop is sown to avoid any contamination of the plants as they grow.

Once seeds are drilled or "broadcast" by spinning, the ground has to be consolidated by rolling it, which prevents slugs from moving along the "tramlines" created during drilling and eating the crop. With cereals it is especially important to cover the seeds with earth to ensure they germinate, and to achieve this a "Cambridge" roller with ribbed wheels is normally used.

An increasing number of crops, not only vegetables, are covered by strips of transparent plastic or fleece during the first few weeks after planting to protect them from cold, frosts and disease. This increased used of plastic sheeting – laid by special machines and normally biodegradable – has changed the nature of the British countryside in recent years.

During the growing period, crops are usually sprayed with insectides and pesticides to kill bugs and weeds. On an organic farm this job is done by pest-eating insects. On larger fields wide rigs with dozens of jets are used to apply these chemicals, and the "tramlines" are used to ensure they are spread evenly.

Bees

The honey bee (*Apis Mellifera*) may be small but it is of crucial importance in the production of crops, fruit and wild plants. So are bumblees and many other insects.

Some crops, such as maize, can be pollinated by wind and some flowers can be pollinated by flies, wasps, butterflies, moths, birds and bats. But because bees are the most important pollinator of all we would not have enough food to eat without them.

Bees are like flying Velcro patches, with pollen being caught in their fuzzy hair. They also carry a static electrical charge, which helps pollen stick to them.

A colony of bees is an intricate social organisation which will act collectively to maintain its existence. Bees do this by laying down stores of pollen and honey to survive the winter.

The colony consists of three types of bee: the queen, a large number of worker bees, (from ten to fifty thousand depending on the time of year) and - in the summertime - hundreds of drones.

The queen is fed and looked after by the other bees as she is essential for reproduction: she hatches from a cell in the hive and reaches maturity in a few days.

After a couple of weeks she leaves the hive for mating flights - she may be mated by as many as fifteen drones. She returns to the hive to lay up to three thousand eggs a day. The bees feed one or more of the worker larvae with royal jelly which produces a young queen.

Bee hives in farmland

UK beekeepers produce around four thousand tons of honey for sale each year, even though this is only twenty percent of the honey we consume in the UK: the rest is imported. Bees also produce beeswax that can be used in candles, polishes and other products.

When the colony in the hive gets overcrowded, especially in hot weather, part of it with the original queen may swarm. Bees increase their numbers by swarming: thousands of bees escort the queen across the countryside looking for a new home.

Over the last few years the UK's bee population has decreased dramatically. This is thought to be due to a parasitic mite, Varroa, which invades bee colonies. Wet summer weather, and the use of some pesticides, may also be a factor.

Cattle

From plodding doe-eyed workers to fiery hoof-stamping bulls, all the domesticated cattle of the world derive from the auroch or wild ox (Bos Primigenius). Aurochs evolved in Asia and migrated into Africa and Europe in the Pleistocene era.

The Auroch or Wild Ox

In Asia and Africa the large-horned wild aurochs became extinct by the fifteenth century BC. The last wild aurochs in Europe only died out in Poland in 1627.

Migrating humans took domesticated aurochs all over the world, and it is from these that British breeds descend. Each region developed its own type of cattle to suit the climate, conditions and availability of feed. Cattle provided meat, milk, hides (leather), tools, and muscle power.

Most cattle are horned, but a few breeds cannot grow horns, and these are called polled. The horned cattle are divided into three groups: short, middle and long-horned.

But most horned breeds have their horn buds removed (disbudded) when they are calves, so now you rarely see a horned animal except for Highland Cattle and Longhorns. The horns are removed to stop the animals hurting each other and to make them easier to handle.

It should also be noted that many of the breeds that are called 'red' range in colour from red to brown.

The rich genetic pool of some twenty-five native breeds has also become vulnerable because of the market-driven need to find the perfect milk or beef breed.

The Friesian had come to dominate the milk industry. It was introduced from the Netherlands because of its high milk yield. Subsequently the Holstein, a slightly larger-boned dairy cow, has superseded the Friesian as the dominant dairy breed.

Artificial insemination is practised widely in the farming industry, so a single bull can

In 1903 this Shorthorn was not dehorned

have a huge number of offspring in a vast area. This can have drastic implications if the bull has a genetic imbalance or undesirable characteristics that spread before they are recognised.

This fast-track method of reproduction does away with the need for a farmer to keep a bull, but by dispensing with the traditional long-term approach to breeding, it inevitably diminishes the diversity of cattle breeds which have adapted so well to different regional conditions – and may be needed in the future.

Beef Cattle

Our history of eating beef goes back thousands of years: archaeologists have found beef ribs in the tombs of the ancient Egyptians as food to help them into the next world.

In Medieval Britain cattle were small, thrifty breeds, about the size of a Shetland pony, that could live on rough grazing. However, the population explosion in the UK from the sixteenth to the eighteenth century had a

Hereford cow and calf being sold at an "on-farm" auction

dramatic effect on beef production, as city dwellers wanted meat.

Beef animals bred in the north and west of England were sent in droves to the Midlands to be fattened on grass and turnips, which had been recently introduced. For the first time animals could be kept through the winter.

From here they were taken by drovers, who walked the animals in herds, to the slaughter houses in London and other big cities. There was also a huge demand for tallow (derived from fat) for candles, so the animals needed to be fatter to fulfil this market. They began to breed from only the best and biggest stock to produce animals with deep bodies and large rumps.

The demand for milk had also increased, leading to more dairy calves being produced. A modern dairy cow calves once a year, producing on average four calves in her lifetime. Only one female dairy calf needs to be kept and reared to become a cow to replace her mother's milk yield, leaving three spare.

Selectively mating the dairy cow with a beef bull results in the spare calves having dual characteristics which make them suitable for beef production.

Female cattle before they have calves are called heifers; males are called bulls unless they are castrated, when they become known as steers or bullocks (in some parts of the country both steers and heifers are referred to as bullocks).

Cows have their first calves when they are two years of age and the gestation period is nine months: they can be mated at any time of the year. In beef herds mating is usually natural: a bull is kept to run with the cows. In many dairy herds AI (artificial insemination) is the preferred method of breeding.

Beef from dairy herds

Cattle that are reared for beef can come from either beef herds or dairy herds, or from a dairy cow mated with a beef bull.

When beef is bred from dairy cattle crossed with a beef bull, the new-born calves are kept with their mothers for the first three days of their lives. This ensures that they receive the first milk which is called colostrum, which contains antibodies, vitamins and minerals essential to protect the calf from disease and enable it to thrive.

After this, milk from the dairy cow is used for human consumption and the calves are removed from their mothers. Males are castrated to avoid having strong tasting meat and to control indiscriminate breeding. They mature slowly over a period of one and a half to two and a half years. They are usually kept in small batches with other calves and are reared on powdered milk, known as milk replacer, until they are weaned at six to twelve weeks old.

Milk can be fed to them either from an automatic dispenser with rubber teats or they are taught to drink from a bucket of milk. Their diet then consists of cereals in concentrated pellet form and some roughage such as hay. They are kept indoors until they are old enough to graze at around four to six months, although they can only be turned out to grass at this age during the summer months.

Where both parents are from dairy herds, the male calves raised for meat are known as

Dairy-cross beef calves

bull beef because they are not castrated. (Many male calves from dairy herds are culled at birth because being born to mainly Holstein/Friesian dairy cows, they have a much lower value as beef) As bulls they put on weight more quickly and they reach slaughter weight at around twelve months to avoid the meat becoming tainted. They are reared on cereal based diets and forage and spend their lives indoors.

Beef Herds

The largest proportion of the beef reared in the UK comes from one and a half million beef 'suckler' cows whose calves are reared for the beef market. The cows are called this because they suckle their own calves until the calves are six to nine months old. Sometimes suckler cows will 'adopt' and rear calves that are not their own. For example calves from a dairy herd kept on the same farm or calves bought from other farmers or from markets.

Beef cattle are grass-fed for as much of the year as possible, depending on weather and ground conditions and the hardiness of the breed. For example, cattle on lowland ground that gets waterlogged in the winter months will be moved indoors until the spring. This is not just for the benefit of the animals but is also to ensure that the land is not overused and turned into a mud-bath by the animals' hooves.

They will usually be fed on home-grown forage crops, hay (dried grass) silage (preserved grass), forage maize and straw. Concentrated cereals may also be given to the cattle containing soya products, maize gluten, sugar beet, and oil-seed rape meal.

Salt, mineral and vitamin licks (animals literally lick them) which are compressed into a bucket or block may also be made available, and fresh water is always provided.

Grazed cattle generally take longer to mature and reach slaughter weight than those fed on concentrates. Some breeds take longer to mature than others. They are killed when they reach two to two and a half years.

The last stage of getting a beef animal ready for slaughter is called 'finishing,' ensuring that the weight, condition and fat content of the animal are correct.

Hanging the meat tenderises it and allows the flavour to develop. The market requirements determine how long the meat is hung: the quicker the turnaround the less expensive the meat will be. A well-hung animal from a traditional breed with a marbling of fat will cost more because of the time taken to mature it.

Cattle Diseases

Bovine Spongiform Encephalopathy, commonly known as BSE or Mad Cow Disease, was confirmed in cattle in 1986. The disease came about because meat and bone meal were included in animal feeds. In turn this caused a devastating and fatal disease in humans, Variant Creutzfeldt-Jakob disease, passed from cattle to humans through infected meat.

Now no farm animals are permitted to eat meat and bone meal. Further precautions were taken to reduce the risk from beef, and any parts of the animal that might contain BSE, such as the brain and spinal cord, are removed from the animal and do not go into our food. Mechanical recovery of meat from the bones of cattle is also banned.

Tuberculosis is an infectious, slow, inflammatory disease which produces nodular swellings with a pus-like centre called tubercles: they can be found in any part of the body.

Tuberculosis in cattle has increased in the last few decades: humans can contract the cattle strain and vice versa. Pigs, birds and other wildlife such as badgers can also be infected. It is possible to test for the disease before it becomes contagious and all cattle are tested by a veterinary surgeon on a regular basis.

TB is a heart-breaking subject to farmers, who sometimes see their prime stock destroyed only for a post - mortem to reveal that their cattle did not have TB at all. It is widely thought that badgers, a protected species, spread the disease to cattle and that they should be vaccinated or culled to try and eradicate it. Some trial vaccination and culling programmes have been carried out but there remains strong opposition to badger culling.

Breeds of Beef Cattle
Aberdeen Angus

This breed was established by lairds and farmers in Scotland who combined the indigenous breeds of cattle known as 'Humlies' (the word means polled) and 'Doddies' (animals with large hairy ears and coats). A herd book was established in 1862 and in 1867 the breed became officially known as the Aberdeen Angus.

It is a most economical breed to rear as the animals are hardy and thrive on rough grazing. The good-natured mothers calve easily and produce vigorous calves keen to suckle.

What they look like
Aberdeen Angus are naturally polled: they are generally black in colour but can be red. They are mild-eyed and compact with a sometimes shaggy coat in winter and are a middle-sized beef breed.

How they are used
Although a smaller beef breed with fine bones, their size can be deceptive when compared with carcass weight and quality. They are early maturing and give prime marbled beef (this means they have small layers of fat running through the meat).

Aberdeen Angus animals are widely crossed with other breeds to improve carcass quality. Because their polled gene is dominant it acts as a dehorner in crossbreds. Aberdeen Angus are exported all around the world to improve beef breeds.

Did you know ?
- Aberdeen Angus has developed into a 'brand' which stands for excellent beef
- Burger chains have introduced the 'Angus Burger' which has become a huge success
- Black and Red Angus are now the most popular beef breeds in the USA

Belgian Blue

In the mid nineteenth century Shorthorn bulls from the UK were exported to Belgium to improve the local red-pied and black-pied cattle of that country. The aim was to create a dual-purpose animal, useful for both milk and meat. Because of the heavier muscling that was being achieved, selective breeding then concentrated on producing a beef animal. In the 1960s the breed started to develop extreme double muscling especially of the shoulders and thighs. Although this characteristic of the Belgian Blue is favoured by butchers as the meat is very lean, it makes calving difficult for pure-bred cows which will often need to undergo caesarean sections.

What they look like

Belgian Blues are large beasts with a small boned carcass rippling with muscles; the rump slopes away from the straight back. The colour ranges from nearly all white, blue, blue-pied and blue roan.

How they are used

They produce lean early-maturing beef. The bulls are used internationally as terminal sires crossed with other breeds of cattle.

Did you know ?

- The double muscle on the Belgian Blue has become a natural development for the breed

- The calves are not born with the double muscle, but it starts to appear at around six weeks of age

Belted Galloway

The Belted Galloway is a more milky strain of the Galloway and the first records of it in Scotland date back to around 1790. It may have resulted as a distinct form of the Galloway when the Dutch Lakenvelder cattle (which is belted) were imported in the seventeenth century. The belted was a rare breed which has gained in popularity. Belted Galloways are affectionately referred to as 'Belties'.

What they look like

The Belted Galloway has a very distinctive broad white band encircling its body, and in cows the udder can be white. The main body colour can be black, red or dun. Like the Galloways they have a thick rain shedding coat.

How they are used

Belties produce good slowly matured succulent beef, and can stay outside all year round on extensive grazing in all weathers. The cows are very long-lived, producing calves into their twenties which also reduces replacement costs.

Because they are so eye catching you often see them in Rare Breeds and Wild Life parks.

Blonde d'Aquitaine

Recognised as a breed in its own right in 1962, the Blonde d'Aquitaine is the result of crossing several Pyrenean breeds, notably the Garonnais and the Quercy. The French have rigorously tested the breed since its conception to evaluate growth rate, lean muscling, proportion of meat to bone and ease in calving. This selective breeding program has resulted in a hardy, docile animal noted for its beefiness and economic value. The breed can now be found all around the world.

What they look like

The Blonde has a golden corn colour with lighter shades around the eyes, muzzle and lower legs. They are a large animal and can be polled or horned. The horns curve forward.

How they are used

They convert food into meat very efficiently to produce lean red beef.

Its light colour, short hair and active sweat glands makes it very heat tolerant and ideal for hot climates.

British White

These handsome striking cattle are thought to have descended from the Wild White cattle of Bowland Forest which was near to the park at Whalley Abbey in Lancashire. They were originally thought to be a polled variety of White Park cattle but it has been shown that they are not closely related. They are classed as a rare breed, although numbers have improved, and they have been exported to America and Australia.

What they look like

The coat is white all over and most commonly with black points, although red or brown points can also occur. The coloured points are on the ears, muzzle, eyelids, teats and feet and there may be a few freckles over the shoulders.

How they are used

The British White were once dual-purpose cattle, but they are now used for high-quality meat and kept as single-suckle beef herds (to rear one calf only). The bulls are sometimes used as crossing sires with dairy cattle.

Did you know ?

- The animal's pigmented skin and white coat, which reflects the sun, make it suitable for hot countries, where it also has a resistance to ticks

- During the Second World War some British Whites were sent to America to ensure the breed survived

Charolais

The Charolais were largely confined to the province of France originally known as Charolais. The area had a good climate and soil and the breed was large and mainly used for meat. Their isolation in this area meant they retained the beef qualities that other cattle lost by being used as draught animals. They developed thick necks and shoulders which resulted in an abundance of cheaper meat cuts. In the mid 1900s they were exported to many countries including the UK where they have remained popular.

What they look like

Charolais are naturally horned, white or cream in colour with a large, deep, broad body. They have a pink muzzle and light-coloured hooves.

How they are used

They are a late-maturing breed, which reach a heavy weight before putting on too much fat, and provide a good beef carcass. They are crossed with dairy cattle to produce beef animals but care has to be taken as calving problems may occur if the bulls are too big.

Did you know ?

- In February 2009 a Charolais bull sold for fifty-five thousand guineas at the Perth livestock auction

- In the 1930s two bulls and ten heifers were exported to Mexico. Until the 1960s all of the Charolais cattle in Mexico, the United States and Canada were descended from this herd

Devon (or Ruby Red)

Devon is the only English county to have two native breeds of cattle. This is because the South Devon and Devon breeds fulfilled different roles - one for milk and one for beef - and they have both survived.

The Devon is a middle-horned, early maturing animal that thrives well on poor grazing and can survive in a hostile environment. It is also one of the most

Did you know ?

• The breed is especially useful in hot climates as the dark pigmentation of the skin protects them from the sun's harmful rays.

• In the 1908 cattle census, Devon or Ruby Reds made up 6.5% of the national herd, the second most numerous breed after the Shorthorn

attractive of our native breeds, and in the eighteenth century the livestock engraver Gerrard described it as "almost the most perfect breed in Britain." The breed originated on Exmoor and is widespread throughout Devon, parts of Somerset and the West Country in general.

What they look like

The Ruby Red is curly coated with a rich, dark-blood colour that blends in with the dark red Devon soil. They are agile, deep-chested and fine-boned, and are very hardy and active. They are generally polled.

How they are used

The Ruby Red is mostly kept as a beef animal. The cows are fertile, good mothers who calve easily and with plenty of creamy milk for their calves. They have also been exported all over the world to improve native breeds of cattle.

Galloway and White Galloway

The south-west of Scotland has been home to this hardy medium-sized hill breed for centuries.

The Galloway was originally a dual-purpose breed used for milk and meat. Cheese and hide were exported from Scotland and later the cattle themselves were moved to fatten on English grass before moving on to Smithfield market. The breed is docile yet fiercely defends its calves from predators.

Cows calve easily and are long-lived. They adapt to differing climatic conditions and are a beef breed which has never been intensively developed. The White Galloway is a dominant colour variation, and like the belted has all the characteristics of the Galloway. They make ideal suckler cows.

What they look like

The Galloways are polled and all have a soft velvety undercoat of hair, with a shaggy thick overcoat of long rain-shedding hairs to protect them from the weather. Their heads and ears are also very hairy, and the switch (tail tip) is long and feathery. Galloways are predominately black with a brownish tinge but they can be red or dun. The White Galloway has a white coat, while its ears, muzzle, eyelashes, knees and feet are contrasted to great effect by being black, red, or dun.

How they are used

Although they are slow growing, the Galloways produce tender, succulent beef. The extra maturing time is compensated by their cheaper production costs as they thrive on rough grazing and stay outside throughout the year. They are often crossed with other breeds such as Shorthorns to achieve a quicker maturing time and to pass on the qualities of good meat and mothering.

Gloucester

The Gloucester is one of the rarest of the dual purpose breeds of the seventeenth and eighteenth centuries when it was highly valued as a dairy cow and also used as a draught animal. The Longhorns and Shorthorns overtook it in popularity and by the early 1900s the breed was almost extinct. A breed society was formed in 1919 to try and increase its numbers, which had fallen to just one hundred and thirty cattle. By 1973 only seventy pure-bred Gloucesters survived. However, with the help of the Rare Breeds Survival Trust, there are now over seven hundred.

What they look like

Gloucesters are a dark mahogany or black colour with a white tail and belly, and a white stripe all along the back bone. They have a short, fine coat of hair and a black tongue and teats. They have middle-sized horns with a black tip that turns upwards.

How they are used

These cattle are famous for producing the milk for Gloucester, Double Gloucester and Blue Vinny cheeses.

As a beef animal they are slow to mature but produce good-tasting fine-grained beef. They are quiet and make good house cows (to provide milk for the family).

Did you know ?

- Single Gloucester cheese can only be officially made in Gloucestershire with milk from pure-bred Gloucester cattle

- Gloucester cattle and their cheeses were first mentioned in documents in the thirteenth century

Hereford

It is generally agreed that the Hereford started around the Welsh borders as a hardy draught animal (one which is capable of pulling heavy loads) whose meat was eaten when its working life was over. In Herefordshire, it is said to have been Benjamin Tomkins (who inherited a cow called Silver and her calf) that fixed the breed type. His son Benjamin the Younger developed and improved the Herefords in the 1760s to be economic feeders of grass and grain yet able to gain weight, to be hardy, prolific and mature early.

At this time they were huge animals weighing three thousand pounds (one thousand three hundred and sixty four kilograms), much bigger than they are today. They have remained docile and are renowned for their longevity, still calving at over fifteen years of age.

Did you know ?

- **Herefords are reared in over fifty countries where their total numbers exceed fifty million**

- **In Roman Britain there were small red cattle and the Herefords may have been descended from these animals**

What they look like

Herefords have a dark red to ochre red coat with some curl in it, with a distinct white face, and white underside of the throat and belly. They may have white on the lower half of their legs and their tail switch (hairy tip). They are a middle-horned breed with short, thick horns that curve down at the side of the face.

How they are used

They are fast-growing cattle who are easy to handle and have been exported throughout the world as they can withstand great temperature ranges. They have greater weight for age than other breeds and provide good quality beef. The cows make excellent suckler mothers who will adopt calves due to their docility.

The Highland

The Highland is the hardiest, and one of the oldest, cattle breeds in Britain. As its name suggests it originated from the Highlands and west coastal islands of Scotland. Breeders have taken great care to retain its original characteristics. It can survive and be productive where other cattle cannot live. These cattle are extremely maternal and protective of their calves. Calves grow rapidly to weaning point and Highlands are long-lived. It has a shaggy inner coat which can grow to over a foot long. The collective name for the Highland is a 'fold' due to the ancient practice of collecting them together in open stone shelters to protect them from wolves.

What they look like

They are handsome cattle, usually a yellowy dun in colour but can also be black, brindle, red and yellow. They have long 'handlebar' horns and their long coats extend to their

Did you know ?

- For breeding purposes, the cattle used to be 'swum' between the islands and mainland of Scotland in waterways known as kyles, and an alternative name for the breed is 'Kyloe'

- If sheep are kept in the same pastures as the Highland cattle it deters predators from attacking them

faces and can become felted during a long winter. They shed their coats in warmer weather, and it re-grows for the colder conditions.

How they are used

The Highland takes a long time to mature and provides distinctively flavoured superb beef which is well worth waiting for. The meat is marbled and nutritious and has a high protein and iron content.

Limousin

The Limousin comes from the central region of France. They were used as draught animals and killed for their meat at the end of their working life. They are now highly prized for their beef and known in France as the 'butcher's animal'. They are a hardy, adaptable and sometimes volatile breed having survived in the poor weather and soil conditions in their native region. They are now common in the UK, and in the 1980s nearly three hundred thousand British cows were artificially inseminated with semen from forty Limousin bulls.

Did you know ?

- In 2012 a pedigree Limousin bull called Fabio set a world record when it was sold for £126,000 at Carlisle in Cumbria

- The Limousin is thought to be the breed depicted in the cave drawings of Lascaux which are around 20,000 years old

What they look like

They are middle horned and have a dark yellow-red coat, with a lighter shade around the eyes, muzzle, inner legs and tail switch. They have thick, short necks with broad, small heads and a very well-muscled rounded rump.

How they are used

They mature early and provide the lean beef that most supermarkets require.

Longhorn

The British Longhorns and Shorthorns were the most important cattle in the 1700s. Robert Bakewell from Dishley in Leicestershire was foremost in selective breeding to produce commercial stock. Before this time cattle had been bred mainly for milk or to pull ploughs. Bakewell wanted a 'butchers' animal due to the increased demand for meat, fuelled by people working in towns during the Industrial Revolution. He crossed various heifers with a Westmoreland bull and came up with the Dishley Longhorn which became called the English Longhorn.

Robert Bakewell's aim was a uniform animal that always provided the goods - in this case beef. The success was phenomenal and it became the dominant English breed overnight. Due to the way it had been bred, the Longhorn lost the ability to produce enough milk, reproduce as efficiently and remain hardy. With Bakewell's death in 1795 other breeders lost interest in the Longhorn and by 1800 it was almost extinct and the Shorthorn had become the popular breed. Today this docile and long-lived animal is one of Britain's rarest breeds.

What they look like

English Longhorns are a light to dark red and brindle sometimes grey with a white finching (line) along the back continuing down the tail. They are large lean, long cattle with outstanding horns that curve downwards around the face to the nose.

How they are used

The Longhorn has a long and level lactation and produces milk with a high butterfat content. In the past they were used for specialist cheeses such as Stilton. They grow quickly and produce superior well-marbled beef.

Did you know ?
- The English Longhorn is not a relative of the American Longhorn which is descended from Spanish stock
- You can now order and buy Longhorn semen online

Lincoln Red

The pied Old Lincolnshire draught shorthorn cattle, which were thought to have been introduced by the Vikings, were crossed with Durham and Yorkshire shorthorn bulls and this resulted in the Lincoln Red. The herd book for this breed was started in 1896 and it was originally a dual-purpose animal, producing both milk and meat.

As a large animal it was able to compete with continental cattle breeds that were imported into Britain in the 1970s and it was crossed with them. The Lincoln Red has survived as a beef breed due to the efforts of its Breed Society and is monitored by the Rare Breeds Survival Trust.

polled gene has been encouraged in Lincoln Reds by selective breeding since 1939.

What they look like

They are a large framed animal, cherry-red all over, with a broad short face and pink muzzle. They can be horned or polled: the

How they are used

These cattle mature early and put on weight quickly and the beef has a good texture and quality. Because of the polled gene the bulls are used as terminal sires with other breeds.

Murray Grey

The Murray Grey originated in New South Wales as a cross between a light roan Shorthorn cow and an Aberdeen Angus bull. The calf was grey. The cow produced twelve more grey calves and the breed was

established by crossing with grey as the dominant colour. A breed society was formed in 1962 as the new breed had become very popular and commercially viable. The breed was imported into the UK in the 1970s. The Murray Grey is a gentle and docile breed, it calves easily and is very adaptable to different climates.

What they look like

The Murray Grey is of moderate size, with a grey, silver or dark grey coat, and is naturally polled.

How they are used

The cows are good milkers and have calves that grow quickly and fatten readily on grass. They produce a high yield of beef without too much fat, making them popular in Japan and other parts of Asia.

Shorthorn

Shorthorn cattle evolved in the eighteenth century from Durham and Teeswater cattle.

The Colling brothers, Richard and Robert, were instrumental in selectively improving the breed. The Collings family continued to develop two types of Shorthorn: one for milk and the other for beef. These remain the distinct types today, although the Dairy Shorthorn can be dual purpose. At this time the Shorthorn became the most popular breed in England and was exported worldwide, where it has had an enormous influence on the development of other cattle breeds. They are docile and adaptable; the bulls are active and long-lived, and when crossed the offspring have a very good rate of weight gain. Despite the breed's former popularity, numbers in the UK have declined dramatically since the 1950s. The Whitebred Shorthorn is a strain of the Dairy Shorthorn which was selectively bred primarily in the Scottish Borders. It is a rare breed and classed as on the critical list by the Rare Breeds Survival Trust.

What they look like
These cattle can be solid red, red with white markings, white or roan. They are large animals with very well developed hind and fore quarters and they have short horns. The Whitebred Shorthorn is white all over with a thick velvety undercoat and outer coat of soft hairs.

How they are used
The beef type of animal grows quickly and they finish early, producing tender and well-marbled beef. The Dairy Shorthorn provides ample good quality milk.

Did you know ?
- The world's first herd book was published for Shorthorns in 1822

- The bull 'Comet' was sold for 1,000 guineas in 1810, the first ever to make this price

South Devon

The large South Devon originated in the South Hams of Devon over four hundred years ago and was a triple purpose breed. They were used to pull ploughs, for their milk and their meat and were spread across most of Devon and Cornwall. At the beginning of the twentieth century the cattle were exported in large numbers, and the milking potential was encouraged. This had an adverse effect on the beef qualities of the animal and from the 1950s it was bred a little shorter in the leg in an effort to restore its value as a beef producer. In 1972 it was classified as a beef breed. The breed is docile, hardy, adaptable and long lived.

What they look like

South Devons are the largest of the British breeds with a medium to yellowish red curly coat. Most are horned but naturally polled animals do occur. They have thick skins which are tinged with yellow and a pink colour around the eyes and muzzle. Their large broad heads lead into a deep full body.

How are they used?

South Devon cattle convert grass into meat very efficiently and mature early to provide good, marbled beef. The bulls are used as crossing or terminal sires (a bull whose offspring is intended for slaughter). The cows, with their ample milk which is rich in butter fat, are kept in suckler herds.

Did you know ?
- South Devons were exported on the Mayflower voyage in 1620
- Unusually, ten percent of South Devon calvings are twins

Sussex

These cattle were widely used as plough ox on the stiff clay wealds of Sussex right into the twentieth century. They are still good quick movers with powerful legs and feet. After their six or seven years as draught animals they would have been slaughtered for meat. Their history as draught animals has bred into them a willingness to be handled and a placid nature. They have been improved as a beef breed by selection rather than crossing and in general have remained in their original regions. The Sussex survives on rough grazing but fattens quickly when moved onto good pasture. The fertile and long-lived cows can calve at two years; have rich but not plentiful milk that is adequate for the small calves which make for easy calving.

Did you know ?
- Unlike other cattle the Sussex does not discriminate when grazing: it eats the whole field, weeds and all, down to an even sward

- They have twice as many sweat glands as other European breeds so adapt well to hot climates

What they look like
They are medium-sized and medium horned with a deep chestnut brown coat and white tail switch. They have become more compact and shorter legged than their draught ancestors.

How they are used
They provide lean, marbled meat especially in the more expensive cuts. Sussex bulls are also used as sires for dairy and suckler herds as they are quick to mature.

Welsh Black (Gwartheg Duon Cymreig)

Although traditionally a dual-purpose milk and meat breed, the Welsh Black is now used mainly as a beef animal. It is thought to be descended from the cattle of Pre-Roman Britain and of other Welsh breeds that have become extinct. Traditionally Welsh women looked after the milking cows which were hand-milked and chosen for their docility.

The cows are excellent mothers with plenty of milk right through their lactation. These cattle are noted for their hardiness and will live outdoors all year round and calve easily. Over time the harshness of the Welsh hills has acted as a natural selector for only the best and strongest mothers of the breed to survive.

Did you know ?

- Occasionally a red recessive gene occurs in a Black herd resulting in red cattle
- The red cattle have no black genes and if they are mated the result is always a red calf
- The breed has been exported in small numbers to Jamaica, Uganda and Saudi Arabia

What they look like

The Welsh Blacks are middle horned with black tips, and have short legs and heads with large docile eyes and large ears. There is also a Polled Welsh Black. Their coats are rusty black to jet black, and they sometimes have a little white underneath behind the navel. They have thick black skin which gives protection from the sun, and their dense coats are quite long and soft. The coat is shed in warmer weather and remains sleek in hotter climates.

How they are used

They are used for beef production on uplands and marginal areas, mostly as pure-bred or cross-bred cows in suckler herds. They produce high quality succulent beef as they gain weight quickly without putting on too much fat.

White Park

Horned 'wild white cattle with coloured points' are mentioned in Celtic and Druidic writings in Ireland and Wales so they are truly an ancient breed. Some of the ancient herds still exist today, including the Welsh Dynevor, the Chartley (originally from Wales but now in Staffordshire), the Scottish Cadzow and the Chillingham in Northumberland.

From the fourteenth century several herds of cattle were enclosed in parkland in Britain - it is thought they were used for sport and because they are such handsome animals. Like the British White a small group were sent to America during the Second World War. They are a rare breed and classed as a critical category because of their low numbers.

What they look like

They have a white coat with black or red points on the ears, muzzle, eyelids, teats and

feet. They have middle to long horns which grow outwards, forwards and then upwards.

How they are used

White Park cattle are hardy, long-lived and adaptable and would be a very useful beef animal if their numbers could be increased.

Vaynol

The Vaynol is listed as 'Critical' by The Rare Breeds Survival Trust; there are around 40 cattle in existence. The herd was established

in 1872 in Vaynol Park, North Wales, where it was semi-feral. In 1980 the herd was moved to several locations in England and then all to Temple Newsham rare breed farm park. In 1999 three cows were moved to a farm in Lincolnshire to reduce the risk of a disease like Foot and Mouth affecting the entire stock.

What they look like

Vaynol are small angular cattle which are all black or white with black points on the ears, muzzle, feet, eyelids and teats. Their horns grow upwards. They have a reputation for being aggressive, and there is a strict hierarchy within the herd.

How they are used

With such low numbers they are kept for exhibition purposes.

Dairy Cattle

The dairy industry has changed dramatically in recent years, with half the number of cows, and only one tenth the number of dairy farms that existed in the 1950s but a threefold increase in milk yield per cow.

Today there are just over two million dairy cows in the UK. The major dairying regions are the South West, the North West and Wales, and we are the third largest producer of milk in Europe. There are around 21,000 dairy farms in the UK, 50% with herds of over one hundred milking cows.

The average yearly milk yield per cow is now about 7000 litres. Due to their high yield, 95% of the national herd are now Holsteins, the remainder being Friesian Jersey, Guernsey or Ayrshire.

Milk from dairy farms in the UK provides around 10% of all food and drink consumed and processed in the country - an annual turnover of around six billion pounds.

Milk production in the UK is limited by quotas (as it is in the rest of the EU) which means each farmer can only produce an agreed amount of milk. The national quota for the UK is 14.2 billion litres, which is divided up between farms. Quota can be bought and sold between farmers just like any other commodity.

How the Dairy Industry developed

Bottled milk was first sold in the 1880s. Urban development and an increasing population created the demand, and the railway system made it possible to get the milk to the masses.

Before the railway provided a link with the countryside, the urban population obtained their milk from cows that were kept in the towns and fed on a diet that consisted mainly of brewer's grains. As soon as their milk yield dropped, the cows were slaughtered.

The warm milk in brass churns was trundled around the streets on carts and was ladled straight into the customer's jug. But as milk began to travel around the country by train, it was important to cool it quickly - as soon the cow was milked - to stop bacteria multiplying.

Milk buckets and churns were left to stand in running water, sometimes streams, to cool the contents. Later on, a dome top was fitted to the churns with holes around the edge overhanging the churn. Hosed cold water came in at the top and trickled down the outside to cool the milk inside.

Milk is highly perishable, especially when warm, providing an ideal host for bacteria to multiply and spread infectious diseases such as tuberculosis and typhoid. In 1886 a German agricultural chemist, Franz Ritter von Soxhelt, proposed that milk should be pasteurised.

Pasteurisation heats the milk to below boiling (71.7 centigrade) which slows

Loading Milk at Aysgarth Station in Yorkshire in 1929

Handmilking cows in 1940

Norfolk milking shed in 1945

microbial growth in foods. It is named after Louis Pasteur who invented the process in 1862 as a way of stopping wine and beer from souring.

Seventeen-gallon churns were used to transport the milk to country railway stations where they were lined up in the shade waiting for the 'milk train'. This gave rise to the 'Express Dairy Company'. The porters had to develop the fine art of rolling the heavy churns on to the trains.

Later on, dairies were built next to many railway stations where milk was bottled and crated before being put on trains and delivery lorries.

The liquid milk industry grew in leaps and bounds in the 1920s and 30s. This led to a chaotic system of producers and dairies undercutting each other. So in 1933 the Milk Marketing Board was formed after a vote in Parliament and it took over the distribution and price regulation of all liquid milk.

The Board collected money from the buyers and made regular payments to the farmers producing the milk, which gave them the security to plan their businesses. The MMB was abolished in 1994 to be replaced by a network of private milk buying organisations.

One problem with the production of milk at that time was ensuring a regular supply throughout the year. Cows generally calved in the spring and produced most milk on summer grazing. Increasingly cows were encouraged to calve in the autumn, their milk yield being sustained by feeding them concentrates.

Artificial insemination gave all farmers access to better breeding stock with potentially higher milk yields. Campaigns began to eradicate Tuberculosis and Brucellosis which are dangerous to both cattle and humans.

Brucellosis was eradicated from the UK in the 1970s and has only reoccurred since in imported cattle. Tuberculosis has proved much more difficult to control. In some parts of the country herds are regularly testing positive to the compulsory TB test. Animals that are proved or thought to be positive are slaughtered. Pasteurisation of milk stopped these diseases spreading to humans.

Most cows are kept in a large barn with a concrete passageway down the centre to collect slurry (urine and faeces), On either side, the building is sectioned into cubicles big enough for the cow to walk in and lie down on bedding or rubber mats, but not turn around. So their dung drops into the central passage which can be pushed clean with a scraper on

Cow and scratching brush

the tractor. Today some cubicle units have automatic scrapers to clean them out.

The transition to milking parlours, and the ability to handle feed and slurry mechanically, reduced labour requirements, so now one person can milk up to two hundred cows.

Young dairy cows, which are called heifers, are put in calf (mated) when they are eighteen to twenty four months old. Artificial insemination is widely used on dairy farms although some farms may keep their own bull. The heifer is in calf for nine months and once she has given birth (calved) she will produce milk.

Only after she has had her second calf will she be called a cow. When the calf is born the mother will lick it to remove the birth fluids, dry it and stimulate the calf to get on its feet and suckle within an hour or so of birth.

The first milk she produces is called colostrum which is very thick and yellow and full of antibodies which are essential to protect the calf from disease. Within a couple of days the heifer will be producing milk (lactating) acceptable for human consumption at which time the calf is taken away from her.

The calf will be reared by the farmer on substitute milk (milk powder) and fed from a bucket or automatic teat system. Several calves are kept together for company and providing they are well fed and looked after they adapt easily.

Female calves are reared on the farm to become future dairy cows (milk replacements) or they may be sold to another farmer for the same purpose. Male calves can be reared for meat (beef or veal) on the same farm or sold. But many are killed at birth as there is no market for them.

Bull calves used to be exported to continental veal farms but exports stopped after the BSE

Modern housing for dairy cattle

outbreak and because UK consumers were concerned at the way calves were transported and veal was reared in Europe.

There is now considerable pressure from farmers and animal welfare organisations for bull calves from dairy herds to be kept and reared in the UK either for veal or beef. This would reduce the number needing to be culled at birth.

By law all calves have to be ear tagged so they can be identified. The ear tag has a code printed on one side to say which farm it comes from, and another number on the other side which identifies each animal.

Most calves are disbudded (dehorned) in the first week which stops the horns growing so they will not hurt each other or humans when they are fully-grown. This procedure is generally carried out with the use of a local anaesthetic. In the dairy herd male calves that are reared for meat are usually left entire (not castrated).

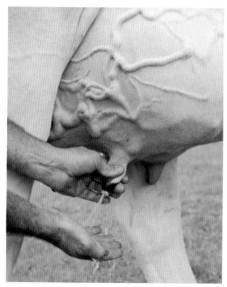

Squeezing milk from a cow's udder

Cows generally have a calf once a year, and are put in calf three months after the birth of their last calf. The cow will keep lactating until about three months before the birth of her next calf when she is 'dried off' (stopped milking) by the farmer so she can have a rest before the next birth and lactation.

In many modern Holstein dairy herds the physical demands placed on cows have unfortunate consequences. Because of the demand for cheap milk, cows have been bred to give more milk at each of their lactations (even though milk-boosting hormones are not used in the UK).

They can find it difficult to consume enough food to support their normal bodily functions, as well as a growing calf and a huge udder full of milk. This has led to them being worn out and sent for slaughter at around five years old, when their natural life span can be around twenty years. The pressure put on the cows can also lead to severe lameness, infertility and mastitis, an udder infection.

Many farmers have become unhappy with the pressure put on their cows and are now importing Swiss Brown cows as an alternative and crossing them with their Holsteins. Swiss Browns are much hardier, well fleshed and have a more even lactation which reduces the stress on them so they will live longer.

Most farms that have solely dairy herds will graze them for the spring and summer. For the remainder of the year they are kept inside in barns. However a small but increasing percentage of dairy farms run on a 'zero grazing' regime.

Cows are kept inside all the year round and fresh grass is cut and transported to them. Keeping cows inside all the year round and depriving them of a natural habitat is not popular with the public and many traditional dairy farmers.

How cows are milked

When cows were milked by hand, one person could hand milk about twelve cows. Then the milking machine was introduced and cows stood side by side in a long shed with a chain around each cow's neck.

The basis of a milking machine is a suction pump which creates a vacuum in a sealed container. Held together with a series of soft rubber hoses the rhythmic sucking and squeezing goes all the way into the soft rubber liners inside the four cups (cluster) that fit on the cow's teats, encouraging her to let the milk down.

A long metal pipe which looks like a water pipe but is actually a vacuum pipe ran at head height above the cows. There was a tap at intervals where the hose from the milking bucket could be fixed to move from one cow to the next. When the heavy milking bucket was full the milk was tipped into a churn to be cooled until all the cows were milked. One person could milk between thirty and sixty cows using a milking machine (see photo on page 86).

But nowadays most cows are milked in a milking parlour, where a limited number of cows enter a special building, stand in their own place, are milked, leave the building and are then replaced by the next batch. (Cows are animals of habit and have their own pecking order.)

The vacuum pump still supplies the power to an enclosed system of glass jars and pipe lines feeding straight into a bulk cooling and refrigerated storage tank. A lorry (milk tanker) sucks the milk directly from an outlet at the bottom of the bulk tank and takes it to the dairy for processing, usually every other day.

In modern milking parlours, the herdsman or herdswoman stands in a pit so the cow's udders are easily accessible for putting the

Modern milking parlour

clusters on. It takes approximately five minutes to milk ten litres from a cow. The udder is washed before milking with a sanitizing solution, which also helps to stimulate the udder to let the milk down.

Four or five squirts of milk are stripped (squeezed) from each quarter (the cow has four teats) into a strip cup to ensure the cow does not have mastitis. After milking, each teat is dipped in a solution which prevents infection in the teat and acts as a skin conditioner to avoid cracked and sore teats.

According to how much milk she is producing, each cow will be given a ration of supplementary feed whilst being milked.

Robotic milking systems, which are used by some large-scale dairy farmers, automatically milk the cows when they want to be milked with minimum input from the farmer.

Bulk milk cooling tank

Breeds of Dairy Cattle

Ayrshire

This breed comes from Cunningham in the County of Ayr and is Scotland's only native dairy cow. They were originally known as Dunlop cattle and were famed for their cheese. As the cattle spread to other areas they became known as the Ayrshire. They are very efficient grazers and foragers able to survive adverse conditions and still be productive. Ayshires are long-lived, of good temperament and calve with ease. Until the 1980s they were second only to the Friesian in the UK in volume of milk produced. The over supply of milk and the rise of the Holstein led to a sharp decline in numbers.

What they look like

The Ayrshire has beautiful lyre shaped horns, although most are dehorned as calves. They are medium-sized cattle of a red, brown and white colour: they may be mostly all white or mostly all red. They have very good udders with the teats evenly spaced.

How they are used

The Ayrshire is an excellent milk cow and bull calves can be raised for beef. The milk is well suited for cheese and yoghurt making.

> **Did you know ?**
> - **The Ayrshire's ability to withstand the cold has made it the preferred breed in Finland where it is called the Finnish Ayrshire**
> - **In Africa it has been crossed with native breeds and the offspring have the ability to produce quality milk on a meagre diet**

British Friesian

Friesian cattle were first brought to the UK from Jutland in the seventeenth century and they take their name from the Dutch province of Friesland. Dutch farmers improved the breed to produce high milk yields, although they are still a dual purpose animal. By the 1940s they had become the most popular milking cattle in Britain due to their high milk production and grazing ability. They also calve more often during their lifetime than other dairy cattle so fewer replacements are needed, and the calves can be reared for meat. Cheaper Canadian and American Holsteins were imported into Britain in the 1970s and were crossed with Friesians to further improve milk production. Many Friesians now have a large percentage of Holstein blood and are losing their dual purpose standing.

What they look like
Friesians are large black and white cattle with a good covering of flesh, and are short-horned. They can also be white with red patches although this is not as common.

How they are used
Milk and milk products, meat from reared and finished Friesian calves, or the cows may be crossed with a beef breed to improve the carcass of their offspring.

Did you know ?
- The once highly regarded Friesian has been largely replaced in the British farming industry by the Holstein
- Today 95% of dairy cows in the UK are black and white

Brown Swiss

In the Swiss Alps monastic records from the Middle Ages show that the Brown Swiss is a very old breed. Its ability to live and graze at such high altitudes has made it a hardy, healthy and adaptable cow. The breed was imported into the UK in the 1970s and is establishing itself as an alternative dairy breed. Other dairy breeds are crossed with Brown Swiss bulls, which passes on the breed's longevity and resistance to disease especially in the legs and hooves. They have very good temperaments and are easy to get in calf.

What they look like
The Brown Swiss has a greyish-brown coat and is a medium size breed with a deep chest and good hindquarters. They are naturally horned and the cows have well attached udders.

How they are used
They are exceptionally good grazers, high yielding milk producers and have a resistance to mastitis. Because they are very well fleshed they have a good carcass value.

Did you know ?
• Brown Swiss milk contains much higher naturally occurring proteins, making it ideal for cheese making

Dexter

The Dexter, which originated in the south western region of Ireland, has been purposefully bred small and there is a dwarfing factor in the breed. The name comes from a Mr Dexter who was agent to Lord Howarden in County Kerry. Mr Dexter developed the breed, probably from mountain cattle, to be small, docile, efficient and suitable as a house cow. They are hardy, intelligent, very easy to handle and because of their popularity are now no longer considered a rare breed.

What they look like

The colour of this breed is predominately black, but can be red or dun. They have horns and are very small, reaching to about waist height. There are two types: one has shorter legs than the other.

Did you know ?

- A Dexter kept as a house cow will give 10 to 12 litres of milk per day

- Dexters are about a third of the size of Friesian cows

How they are used

They are dual purpose and ideal as a smallholder's cattle providing rich, easily digestible milk and beef.

They mature early and the beef is produced economically and is of a high quality and flavour. Dexters are also kept as pets and being small do not churn up the land.

Guernsey

The Guernsey probably originated from a French breed of cattle called the Froment du Leon which came from Brittany. During the eleventh century Norman monks brought cattle with them and settled in Alderney and Guernsey. They were thought to have crossed their imports with Alderney cattle which are now extinct. Guernseys were kept pure because further imports to the islands were restricted. They came over to England in the seventeenth century and were renowned for their rich, plentiful milk. In the twentieth century the Guernsey was highly valued as a commercial milking cow.

Did you know ?

- Because of their rich yellow milk they are sometimes known as the 'Golden Guernsey'

- The Guernsey used to be kept as an ornamental breed on the great estates

What they look like

They are a short-horned medium-size breed. The coat is golden to reddish-brown with white patches, and the muzzle and feet are buff coloured.

How they are used

The Guernsey provides milk with a good butter fat content.

Holstein

The Holstein, which orginated 2000 years ago in the Netherlands on either side of the Zuider Zee, is Britain's dominant dairy cow.

In the nineteenth century the Canadians and Americans imported large numbers of the cattle as they were impressed by their milking qualities. The Americans concentrated on improving the breed just for milking.

In 1967 an outbreak of foot and mouth in the UK caused the culling of many dairy herds and these were replaced with Canadian Holsteins. Artificial insemination is used in the dairy industry worldwide, and popular Holstein sires dominate the breeding, leading to a very narrow genetic base. This can cause genetic defects, and problems such as low fertility in some Holsteins.

What they look like

Holsteins are big full boned animals. They are black and white, sometimes red and white, with a predominance of white.

How they are used

Some Holstein cows can produce almost ten thousand litres of milk a year, which is more than any other dairy breed. The physical demand of carrying this much weight and having to eat so much to sustain the output, has led to lameness, which means ranging for grass is difficult, and mastitis is common which has to be treated with antibiotics. These demands shorten the cow's life so Holsteins are mostly worn out by the time they are five years old and are sent for slaughter. The meat is used but it is not of a high quality.

Did you know ?

- **The average milk yield per cow in the 1970s was around 3750 litres, while today it is in the region of 9000 litres**

- **A bull called Picston Shottle has become the first UK bred sire to produce over one million doses of semen in his lifetime**

Irish Moiled

The Irish Moiled is rare and was traditionally a dairy cow; it has evolved as a dual-purpose breed. By the 1970s the breed had less than thirty females remaining in Ireland. With the help of the Rare Breeds Survival Trust and dedicated breeders the numbers have increased to around one hundred. The cows calve easily and will continue to breed until they are up to fifteen years old. The breed is easy to handle

including the bulls which have a good temperament, and will out-winter.

What they look like

The Irish Moiled are naturally polled and are red in colour, with white markings especially along the back, which is referred to as 'flinching'. They often have white on the underbelly and tail and the head is quite mottled and lighter in colour than the body.

How they are used

The cows give a good yield of milk, and are also used in suckler herds, where they raise calves exceptionally well. Their beef is of the highest quality with a superb distinctive flavour.

Did you know ?

- The word moiled comes from the Gaelic word 'maol' or 'maoile' literally translated as 'little mound' and simply means the animal is polled or hornless

Jersey

The Jersey is a very agreeable and special breed thought to be descended from Asian ancestors, and then brought to Jersey by migrants when it was still joined to France. For the last two centuries the breed has developed in isolation on the island of Jersey, as no imported cattle have been allowed in. By contrast the export of pure Jersey cattle from the island has been huge and to all parts of the world. This is due to the animal's amazing ability to adapt to extreme climatic conditions, especially heat, and to resist disease. The cows are docile, respond well to gentle handling and make good house cows although the bulls can be aggressive and spiteful.

What they look like

Most Jerseys are a light honey brown, though shades can range from almost black to greys and fawns. They have black feet and a black nose with a white halo surrounding it, a slightly dished face, wonderful soft, doe eyes with long lashes and short horns. As one of the smaller breeds they are dainty and noble.

How they are used

Jerseys are used for their milk which is almost unique as it contains much higher levels of calcium, protein and butterfat than that from other breeds. Although due to their size they produce less milk than Friesians or Holsteins, because of its quality when converted into cheese and other milk products, it is of equal or even greater value.

Did you know ?

- Although Jerseys make up only around 2% of the British milk herd, worldwide they are the second largest breed of milk cow

- Jersey dams are much more likely to adopt other cow's calves and rear them as multiple sucklers

Kerry

Thought to be one of the oldest breeds of cattle in Europe, archaeological evidence suggests they have been in Ireland for four thousand years. The Kerry was being bred by and provided milk for early Irish Celts and is probably the oldest specialist dairy breed. They are very hardy as they survive on poor grazing and are ideal for hill farms. In Ireland they have been known as the poor man's cow because of their small size; yet the English imported them as ornamental animals for their estates in the 1800s. Although they are no longer treated as a rare breed they neared extinction in Ireland in the 1980s.

What they look like

The Kerry is black with fine bones and middle-sized white horns with black tips which curve upwards. She is the ballerina of

the bovine kingdom with her pert head and graceful carriage.

How they are used

She is an economical producer of top class milk with a high yield in comparison to her size. The milk has small fat globules which make it very digestible. The steers will fatten for beef although they take about six months longer than other breeds.

Red Poll

These cattle were native to East Anglia, particularly Suffolk, where they did well on poor sandy land. The Red Poll, a dual purpose breed, is thought to have come from the crossing of the Norfolk Red, a meat breed, and the Suffolk Dun, a milk type, in the 1800s.

During the 1950s it was a prominent breed in the UK due to its ability to produce good meat and milk on home-grown feed. With a growing preference for the Friesian, although it had to be fed on concentrates, the demise of the Red Poll was inevitable. Despite its ability to thrive on cheap rations the numbers became so low that it was classified as a rare breed.

What they look like

As the name suggests they are polled, of medium size and the coat is a rich dark red with a white tail switch. They usually have a red udder, with sometimes a little white on the inside flank.

How they are used

They are used for their high quality meat and milk. The milk is very digestible as it has small fat globules and makes good cheese. The cows are suited to suckling more than one calf.

Did you know ?
- The cow will produce calves when they are fifteen or more years of age

- Although we no longer value the Red Poll in Britain, its tolerance in hot or cold conditions has led to the breed being popular in many other countries

Shetland

Because the British Isles are surrounded by numerous islands some minor cattle breeds developed in isolation, although few of these breeds still survive. The Shetland, though low in numbers, has survived. Its lineage is thought to go back to the Vikings. In 2000 the Shetland Breeders Association was formed to draw attention to its plight and its qualities, in order to prevent extinction. The Shetland is exceptionally hardy, thrifty, long-lived and easy to handle.

What they look like

They are small, fine-boned and solid cattle with short horns and a slightly dished face. Their colour is normally black and white pied, though red and white does occur. In the winter the coat is long and thick but is shed for the summer leaving them sleek and glossy.

How they are used

Shetlands are a dual purpose breed giving a good yield of milk and providing an early maturing succulent beef.

Did you know ?
- In 1983 a herd of Shetlands were exported to the Falkland Islands, being well able to withstand the climatic conditions there

Pigs

Pig production in Britain used to be a 'cottage industry'. During the Second World War, for instance, keeping a pig in the 'back yard' was encouraged because at this time of food shortage it was a good way to convert swill and other waste products into human food.

The pig keeper wanted to rear as many healthy piglets as possible on an inexpensive diet. Traditionally a sow would rear twelve or so piglets a year and these would be weaned at around eight weeks. Most of the piglets were 'reared-on' in outdoor systems with shelters which could be moved around to provide fresh grazing and foraging areas.

The piglets grew at their own rate and were slaughtered when they reached two hundred pounds or more: at this time a 'fatty' carcass was considered an advantage.

The characteristics of the traditional breeds suited the regional markets (for pork and bacon) and the local rearing systems. Pedigree breeds were quite often crossed, for example the Large White was mated with Essex and Wessex sows for bacon production.

In 1949 the first Danish Landraces were imported into Britain. The breed became well established here and was considered to produce a much better carcass, one that has a higher meat to fat ratio.

Pig in watery Heaven

At around this time, pig breeds such as the Yorkshire Blue and White, the Cumberland, the Dorset Gold Strip, the Lincolnshire Curly Coated and the Large White Ulster became extinct. This was because the new imports were considered more commercially viable.

The Hampshire, Duroc, and most recently the Pietrain pig were imported, and included in the UK breeding programme. Commercial artificial insemination was introduced by the Wall's Meat Company which also became the dominant buyer of pigs in Britian.

For over a century pure-bred British pigs have been the building blocks of improving pig breeding around the world.

Generations of farmers bred from the best pigs from within their own pedigree herds to establish and improve regional pig breeds and fierce rivalry between farmers at livestock competitions helped this process.

In the early part of the twentieth century, the Government brought in a system of licensing boars (male pigs) that were to be sold for breeding and they all had to be pedigree registered, to maintain the high standards of each breed.

Plastic buttons or metal tags placed in a pig's ear carry a unique number specific to each animal, in addition to the identification number of the herd and farm. This ensures traceability of every pig living or slaughtered in Britain, a process which is essential if diseases such as swine flu and foot and mouth are to be kept under control.

In the 1960s 'technology' became the buzz word, and progeny testing programmes were set up to evaluate performance and carcass quality for commercial pig production. The piglets were weaned earlier, at five or six weeks old, and farrowing crates and creep feeding were introduced. Sows were now producing up to twenty piglets a year.

Farrowing crates are designed to stop the sow lying on her piglets as they learn to escape under the bars. Creep feeding allows the piglets to feed alone by giving them access to food through a small gap not large enough for the sow to enter.

Indoor Production

The introduction of more intensive pig units in the 1960s enabled one person to look after a very large number of pigs. Large fattening piggeries had a central feeding passage for the whey and barley meal on which pigs were fed. Dung was collected in the outside passages and these were large enough to be scraped clean with a tractor.

Further intensification led to hangar-size concrete pig units housing hundreds of pigs in pens on bare concrete and slatted floors. Slatted floors allow the muck and urine to drop through and this is then pumped to a slurry lagoon so it can be spread on the land during dry weather.

Sows were put to (mated with) the boar when they were about eight months old.

Farrowing crate

Intensive pig unit

During pregnancy sows were tethered or kept in stalls so that they could lie down or stand up but not turn around, and the piglets weaned at three weeks.

Pigs are naturally intelligent, boisterous and playful animals designed for foraging. Keeping them in such an intensified way leads to boredom, which in turn leads to tail and ear biting and a variety of illnesses. Consequently antibiotics were routinely administered to piglets which had their tails docked and teeth clipped. They were housed in semi-darkness to keep them calmer.

Now, although there are still some intensive pig units in the UK, increased standards of animal welfare have been demanded by the consumer which has resulted in better husbandry.

Stalls, tethers and the routine use of antibiotics are banned in this country and all medicines administered to the pigs must be logged in a medicines record book. The re-invention of outdoor pig keeping means you see many more pigs rooting around the countryside. The high cost of indoor pig housing and planning regulations have also had an impact.

Two Tamworth sows on straw

A newly-born piglet

Pigs can also be loose reared on straw in large open-sided sheds that let in the daylight. Farrowing crates (which are slightly larger than stalls) are still allowed to be used for a maximum period of four weeks and they do prevent piglets from being squashed by their mothers. Indoor systems do generally still dock tails and clip teeth when the piglets are a day old.

Outdoor Production

Outdoor units are ideally sited on free draining soils, as piglets are born all the year round. Heavy soils become waterlogged in the winter which can lead to high piglet mortality. In summer pigs can suffer from sunburn so trees or sunscreens provide shade. Providing a waterhole for the pigs to wallow in means they coat themselves with mud which helps to protect them from the sun's rays.

Six to eight pigs are kept on an acre and they are moved from one area to another and kept in with electric fencing. Straw filled moveable arcs, often semi-circular with a solid back and door at the front, are used as living and farrowing quarters and are spread across a field. Manure from the pigs goes directly back onto the soil, acting as a fertiliser and does not have to be disposed of separately.

Although forty per cent of all breeding sows are kept outdoors only a tiny percentage of their piglets, which are weaned at three weeks, are reared and fattened outdoors. In order to survive piglets must have colostrum from their mothers within a few hours of birth to help their immunity systems: a piglet always returns to the same teat to suckle.

Male piglets are not castrated in the UK and meat from boars slaughtered at heavier weights can become tainted. It is generally tested at the abattoir to make sure it has no odour.

Piglets still with their mother

At weaning piglets are moved into indoor pens on straw to fatten up. This leads to confusion for the consumer who might quite naturally assume a label claiming 'outdoor bred' is the same as 'outdoor reared'. After the piglets are weaned the sow has a break of one week before she commences heat (oestrus), and is put to the boar or artificial insemination again.

Outdoor and indoor pigs are fed on processed food pellets made up of cereals and vegetable proteins such as soya beans. Smaller pellets are fed to the piglets after weaning. By law all pigs must have access to water and a minimum of one drinker per fifteen pigs is required for indoor units.

The drinkers are usually nozzles protruding from the wall from which the pigs suck water. The pig farmer must ensure there is two days' reserve of water.

Outdoor rearing in Norfolk

Organic Production

Pigs have free access to open fields and they sleep in straw-filled arks. In organic

Middle White piglets enclosed by electric fence

systems, stocking rates are much lower, farrowing crates are not used, and weaning occurs at eight weeks. This allows the piglets to become much stronger, doing away with the need for antibiotics, tail docking and teeth clipping.

The pigs are fed on organic supplementary feed and in mixed-farms form part of the agricultural cycle by rooting out the ground, fertilising it and making it ready for a new crop, such as corn. The cost of raising organic pork products is almost double that of conventional systems.

UK welfare systems for pig keeping are far in advance of most other countries. This increases the cost of pig production in the UK and leads to cheap imports which undermine our own pig farmers.

Pig Breeds

Berkshire

The original Berkshire was a reddish colour spotted with black, larger than the breed of today and came from the Thames Valley. In the 1800s Lord Barrington introduced Chinese and East Asian blood to improve the breed.

Cromwell's army are said to have discovered the Berkshire when quartered at Reading, and Queen Victoria owned a boar named 'Ace of Spades' which was the first Berkshire ever recorded.

What they look like
A black pig with a white blaze on the face and four white feet. The tip of the tail is white.

How they are used
They are traditionally a pork pig, which finish early at around 35 kilograms. The meat has a distinct flavour with wonderful 'crackling.' The Berkshire carcass dresses out completely white, is of a fine texture, with a large proportion of lean meat to fat and a superb flavour of its own. It is another pig that almost became extinct due to the demand for leaner meat. Happily a few enthusiasts ensured its survival, and it is found in small specialist herds in the UK

British Landrace

The British Landrace Pig was first imported into Britain from Sweden in 1949 and was part of the first Pig Testing Scheme in the UK which recorded daily weight gains and fat depths. The Landrace is one of the most popular commercial breeds and has been developed for speed of growth to supply a long lean carcass. They are found throughout the UK, mostly in large commercial herds. Ninety per cent of crossed pig production in Western Europe and America use Landrace bloodlines.

What they look like
The Landrace is a large white pig with a fairly straight nose that turns slightly concave with age and medium-size ears that droop and slant forward. The pig has soft skin which is slightly pink with fine white hairs. The tail is curly and set high.

How they are used
They are used both in indoor and outdoor systems, and prized for a good fleshed lean carcass which is ideal for bacon or fresh pork.

British Lop

For the first half of the twentieth century the British Lop remained in its local area around Tavistock on the Devon and Cornwall border. It was well adapted to the locality and suited the regional markets. In 1973 the Rare Breeds Survival Trust listed the British Lop as rare, which drew attention to the breed and made it more popular. The Lop is docile, hardy and a very good mother with plentiful milk.

What they look like

The Lop is a large long pig with a white coat of fine long hairs and lop ears. Until the 1960's when its name changed to the British Lop, it was known as the National Long White Lop Eared Breed.

How they are used

The British Lop is a good grazer and can be kept outside all year round so they are

suitable for smallholders and for extensive commercial systems. The pork and bacon from the Lop is of high quality, has a niche market and the pig does not tend to run to fat.

British Saddleback

The Essex pig mainly found in East Anglia and the Wessex pig from the New Forest were crossed to produce the British Saddleback which was established in 1967. Saddlebacks are hardy, good grazers noted for their mothering ability. They are widespread throughout the UK. The sow below has cross-bred piglets.

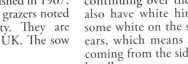

What they look like

Saddlebacks are black with a band of white extending over the shoulders and continuing over the forelegs. They may also have white hind feet and tail and some white on the snout. They have lop ears, which means they cannot see you coming from the side, and so are easier to handle.

How they are used

Saddlebacks are used for pork, bacon and as heavy pigs. They are quite often crossed with other breeds and have a niche market. Supermarkets looking for ultra-lean carcasses were instrumental in the decline of the breed to the extent that in 1979 it was placed on the rare breed list.

Duroc

The Duroc originated in America in the early 1800s where they were known as "Red Hogs". Today's Duroc evolved from crossing Red Durocs from New York with Jersey Reds from New Jersey. The Duroc is named after a famous trotting stallion which was owned by breeder Harry Kelsey of Florida

Durocs tend to be aggressive and not very good mothers. They are usually crossed with white pigs to take advantage of their mothering abilities whilst still providing the quality meat associated with the Duroc. They have a niche in the UK pig sector in outdoor pig production

What they look like

The breed has a distinctive red/auburn coat, hard skin and moults in the summer leaving them bald. They are able to withstand cold, wet and sunshine without adverse effects. They are large framed, muscular pigs with drooped ears.

How they are used

As a purebred they are famed for their bacon. Crossbreds are used for pork or heavy hogs.

Gloucestershire Old Spots

The first recorded spotted breed, it originated by the River Severn in the Berkeley Vale. It grazed in the cider orchards, getting fat on windfalls and the waste from dairy farms, so was known as the Orchard pig. Its spots are said to have come about when the pig was bruised by falling apples!

The pig is quiet to handle and very hardy so ideally suited to outdoor systems. Gloucestershire Old Spots are kept in specialist herds. The breed is going from strength to strength after a previous decline.

What they look like

The Gloucestershire Old Spots are a large white pig and must have at least one clearly defined black spot. Their lop ears almost cover their entire faces.

How they are used

The breed produces top quality meat for all pork cuts and sausages and is in great demand.

Hampshire

The Hampshire was originally a native British breed which was exported to the United States of America in 1832.

In the seventeenth century they were renowned for their bacon and were particularly associated with the New Forest, grazing on acorns and beech masts (fruit). However they were not considered to be of any great merit and were overtaken by other breeds. They were imported back to the UK in 1968 and now considered one of the world's most important breeds.

What they look like

The Hampshire is a black pig with a whitish belt around its body covering the front legs. They have prick ears which is characteristic of the Shire breeds. In America they were known as 'The Thin Rind' breed because they were so lean.

How they are used

They are used as sires for crossbred pigs for the pork and pork processing markets. They produce a lean carcass and are often the prize winner in competitions. Originally, dressing a Hampshire pig involved burning the hair off the carcass instead of removing the hair by scalding, resulting in a completely different flavour to the meat.

Kune Kune

The Kune Kune is a feral pig that lived with the Maori tribes in New Zealand. The breed almost became extinct in the 1970s until two wild life enthusiasts bought eighteen pigs. The population of the Kune Kune in New Zealand is now healthy. They arrived in Britain in the early 1990s.

What they look like

A small pig, only knee height, their colour ranges from cream to black, brown to spotted. They have prick ears. Their name means fat and round in Maori.

How they are used

They are mainly kept as pets but can be eaten. Kune Kune are often seen in 'pets corners' at agricultural fairs and shows.

Large Black

At the beginning of the twentieth century Large Blacks were found all over Britain. A Large Black sow won the Supreme Championship at the Smithfield show in 1919 and went on to sell for seven hundred guineas.

The largest pig in this country, they originate from the Old English Hog. As with other coloured breeds, discrimination against its colour led to the Large Blacks' decline in the 1960s. Some small pedigree herds established before World War II had survived, enabling the breed to continue and it is now found throughout the British Isles. These pigs are docile and are renowned as good, milky mothers.

What they look like

These large all-black pigs have a long body and lop ears. Their ears hang to each side of the face and are so large that they almost obscure the pig's view.

How they are used

The succulent meat is used for bacon and pork. As a traditional breed reared outdoors they are having a revival in popularity.

Large White

The Large White became established in 1868 and is thought to have developed from the Yorkshire breed. Recognised for their ability to cross with and improve other breeds, they were exported to many countries including Russia, Canada and Argentina. Large Whites are found throughout the UK and in many parts of the world. They have been exported to over sixty countries, and are often claimed to be the world's favourite breed.

What they look like

Although called white they look pinkish, have large, long bodies with fine white hairs, dished faces and prick (sticking up) ears.

How they are used

The pigs grow rapidly and the high proportion of lean meat in the carcass makes them very popular in intensive production systems. The meat is used for all types of pork, bacon and pork products.

Middle White

In 1852 Joseph Tulley, a weaver from Keighley in Yorkshire, accidentally established the Middle White breed. He entered his pigs in the Large White class of the local show and the judges deemed them too small for this class and too large for the Small White class. However the pigs were of such outstanding quality that after lengthy discussion the judges decided to create a new class, named the Middle Whites.

The Middle White is a very friendly, docile animal which makes it an ideal choice for the first time pig keeper. After a decline it is now widespread in small herds.

What they look like

Middle White pigs have dished faces and their medium-sized short snout is completely white with fine hairs. They have prick ears which are rather bat-like and fair thin skin which is easily sunburned.

How they are used

The Middle White is an excellent early-maturing pork pig. They are a favourite with good chefs and butchers for their quality and darker meat. The Japanese are very fond of the Middle White and refer to them as the 'Middle York's'

Mangalitza

The Mangalitza or Woolly pig was originally from Hungary. The breed is dispersed around Europe and came to the UK in 2006. They are hardy, friendly and make good mothers. A rare breed, in 1993 there were only one hundred and fifty sows world-wide. Thanks to dedicated breeders they are now in recovery.

What they look like

They have three colour lines "The Blonde", "The Swallow Bellied" and the "Red". They are all curly coated.

How they are used

The Mangalitza has a high level of monounsaturated fat and is used in speciality hams and salamis. They produce good, moist marbled pork. Their curly coats used to be sheared to make men's sweaters.

Oxford and Sandy Blacks

One of the oldest British pig breeds, the Oxford and Sandy Blacks have almost reached extinction on two occasions. In the 1940s only one or two boars were licensed as pedigree each year. The Breed Society has succeeded in keeping some of the rarest bloodlines although the numbers are small. The pig was also known as the 'Plum Pudding' and 'Oxford Forest' pig.

They are a hardy, good tempered pig, not prone to sunburn. Traditionally they were kept by cottagers (country people who live in cottages). Believed to have developed in Oxfordshire about two hundred years ago they are mostly found in small outdoor herds around the British Isles. They are sometimes crossed with white pigs to produce commercial hybrids.

What they look like

One of the most attractive of pigs, they are medium to large with a slightly dished muzzle and semi-lop ears. They are a sandy colour with random black splashes and have white feet with a white blaze and tassel (the tip of the tail).

How they are used

The Oxford and Sandy Black can produce superb white-skinned pork in twenty two weeks and good bacon and ham.

Pietrain

The Pietrain is a minority breed in Britain and comes from a village in Belgium after which it is named. It first appeared in England in 1964. It is used extensively in Spain and Germany as a terminal sire.

What they look like

They are of a medium size and are white with black spots (known as piebald) and have erect ears.

How they are used

They are used in crossbred and terminal sire lines and have a high, lean, meat content. The Pietrain was used by the Walls company in breeding trials.

Tamworth

The Tamworth is the oldest pure English breed descended from The Forest pig. It stayed pure because it was not a fashionable breed during the period when pig improvement occurred and was not crossed with other breeds or developed commercially.

It is hardy and is an ideal free ranging breed as the excellent mothers are also very

protective. The Tamworth is on the Rare Breeds Survival Trust's list and during the 1970s the Trust imported a number of Tamworths to Britain from Australia to boost numbers. Today it is predominantly found in small specialist herds.

What they look like

They are an easily recognisable golden-red medium size pig, with flesh coloured skin. With a slightly dished face they have large prick ears with a fine fringe and their well tasselled tail is set high. The Tamworth has a very inquisitive nature and can run very fast. It is more resistant to sunburn than other native breeds.

How they are used

The Tamworth was traditionally kept to cure for bacon and hams. They are white-fleshed and good for pork. They are often crossed with wild boar to produce a distinctive flavour meat.

Vietnamese Potbellied Pig

They are a descendent of the 'I' breed of pig originating from Vietnam. Although they are small they are able to interbreed with any breed of pig, if they can reach! These pigs are grazers and should have access to grass.

What they look like

They are a small pig with a sway back and a large (potbellied) stomach. They are generally black in colour with prick ears and a straight tail.

How they are used

They are mostly kept as pets. They may live to up to thirty years of age and can be house trained!

Welsh

References to the Welsh pig go back to the 1870s, and it is currently considered 'vulnerable' by the Rare Breeds Survival Trust. But only fifty years ago the Welsh pig was the third most popular sire breed in the UK. The Welsh were part of the national testing scheme in the 1960s and 70s and were widely used in commercial herds as their carcass was ideal for bacon and pork.

They are found in small herds in Wales and other parts of the UK. They are hardy and will thrive indoors or outside and are easily managed.

What they look like

The Welsh is white and has a long, level body. They have lop ears which meet at the tips just short of the pigs snout. The curly tail is carried high. The founder of the modern Welsh breed, George Ellington, described the perfect Welsh pig as "pear shaped".

How they are used

The pigs fatten quickly on less food than most breeds. They produce a good percentage of meat and are commonly used for pork and bacon and still play a role in crossbreeding programmes.

Great escape

Sheep

The humble sheep has had more impact on the British Isles than any other animal. From before the Middle Ages the wealth of the nation was built on wool. Our flocks provided us with clothing, food, employment and valuable exports.

Many towns and personal fortunes were founded on the "back of a sheep", which in turn led to the building of churches, schools, bridges and town halls.

In Parliament the Lord Chancellor still sits on a Woolsack in the House of Lords. This custom was introduced by King Edward III (1327-77) and the red cloth cushion was stuffed with English wool as a reminder of the country's source of wealth, the wool trade.

In summer there are around thirty million sheep and lambs grazing on approximately 82,000 farms and smallholdings. Our national flock consists of some seventy pure native breeds that have adapted to different environments and microclimates, soil types and pasture.

About two thirds of the national flock is found in upland or mountain areas with poor grazing, which would not be suitable for other agricultural purposes. The stocking rate is low, for example one ewe (female breeding sheep) to the hectare. This is known as extensive grazing.

Sheep farmed in lowland areas are stocked at more *intensive* rates of up to twenty ewes per hectare because the grazing is better.

Feeding hay in bad weather. Note the green raddle dye on the sheep's rump

The major breeds of sheep in the UK can be classified into three groups: Mountain and Moorland, Longwools and Lowland flocks.

Mountain and Moorland are collectively known as Upland sheep which are small and able to withstand harsh weather conditions and survive on poor grazing. They are very important in maintaining the landscape and are used to manage heather moorland and other areas.

The flocks are not fenced in and over generations have become 'Hefted' or 'Heafed' which means they are aware of their own home ground and range only in that area.

Once the shepherd would have taken a flock of sheep to a certain area of the uplands and stayed with them for several weeks until they grew to know their boundaries – an area of unenclosed land attached to a particular farm.

Over the centuries this homing instinct has been passed down through generations of ewes who have taught their lambs which land they belong to. They will stay there unless herded in for lambing or shearing.

The collective term for hefted sheep is a 'heft' and if a farm has to be sold the heft is normally sold with it.

Longwools are larger in size and require better quality grazing than other breeds and were originally kept for their wool. *Lowland* sheep are also larger than Upland sheep and are earlier maturing on lush pastures.

Upland and lowland sheep are linked by staged breeding systems, known in farming as stratification. The breeds are mainly kept in the local environments to which they are adapted and are linked together by the movement of lambs and older ewes from the upland to the lowlands.

Lambs from the uplands that do not need to be kept as flock replacements are taken to the lowlands as store lambs to be fattened for meat. Older ewes are also taken down to milder climates to continue breeding.

By crossing pure, hardy hill sheep with Longwool varieties such as Border Leicester, half-bred and *mule* ewe lambs are produced. In turn these are sold to lowland farmers who then cross them with, for example, a terminal Suffolk ram, to produce good fast fattening lamb for meat.

A terminal sire is one that has good meat qualities and is crossed with a ewe of another breed to produce lambs that are specifically for slaughter. The ram (male) lambs from the cross breeding are sold as stores and fattened in the lowlands. By crossing sheep in this way the lambs produced are much more vigorous. British sheep can be found throughout the world because of their diversity and ability to produce good meat as well as wool, and they have been used as foundation breeding stock in many countries.

Upland sheep on extensive grazing

Lowland sheep and lambs

Ewes are seasonal breeders which are usually mated naturally in the autumn with a ram. On lowland farms one ram is kept to around fifty ewes; on hill farms one ram serves twenty five ewes. In big flocks there will be several rams, not necessarily all of the same breed. A few very specialist pedigree flocks may use artificial insemination to be sure of introducing or continuing a particular bloodline.

The gestation period in sheep is twenty one weeks and lambs are mostly born to coincide with the growth of new spring grass. But because of the demand for lamb for the Easter meat trade, some farmers have changed their mating season to July or August so that lambs are born in December and January.

Lambing

During mating rams may wear a harness containing a dye stick or have raddle (dye) painted on their chests. The different coloured dye rubs off onto the ewe's rump, so the farmer can tell when a ewe has been mated, and with which ram.

Rams are kept with the ewes for only a few weeks during the mating season, so the lambing period is limited.

In lowland areas ewes are often scanned to see how many lambs they are carrying. It is common for ewes to give birth to twins – or "doubles" as they are known in farming.

Scanning is helpful as a ewe with three lambs will need more nourishment than a ewe with one or two lambs to ensure that she has plenty of milk for them. Extra feed is normally given in the last six weeks of pregnancy, and supplementary minerals in blocks or buckets are available for the sheep to lick.

Good husbandry to ensure the survival of lambs is critical to the success of sheep farming. As they near lambing time the ewes are brought close to the farm either in sheltered fields or barns, so that assistance can be given with difficult lambing.

Both approaches have their advantages. Lambing outdoors minimizes the chance of infection in a flock. However, bad weather and the possibility of foxes and badgers stealing lambs, mean housing the flock inside may be safer.

Crows and buzzards can also cause problems. Crows will peck lambs' eyes out, and do the same to an immobile ewe. Buzzards will sometimes carry off a whole lamb for a meal.

When a ewe is very close to lambing she will move away from the flock and find a quiet place in which to lamb. When labour starts the ewe may paw and sniff the ground, often turning around, and getting up and down. The lamb can be born when the ewe is lying down or standing up.

Lambs are sometimes presented for birth with a 'leg back' or 'breech' and without assistance from the shepherd both ewe and lamb could die. They should be born with both front legs forward and with the head between them. Once the head and shoulders come out, the rest of the lamb is born very quickly.

The mucus membrane often covers the lamb's face when it is born and the ewe will start to lick this away and dry the lamb. This is an important time for the shepherd to be on hand as lambs can suffocate in the membrane if it is not quickly cleared.

The licking will reinforce the bond and smell between them and stimulate the lamb to get up. Once the lamb is on its feet, it starts to look for milk and its mother will lick and nuzzle it in the right direction for her udder.

If the ewe is carrying a second or third lamb they will be born very soon after the first. The remains of the umbilical cord are still attached to the middle of the lamb's belly, but will wither naturally in a few days. The shepherd will spray or dab iodine (or an equivalent) on the navel of each lamb to prevent infection.

The afterbirth remains trailing from the ewe for a little while after the lambs are born.

A lamb being born

Licking the lamb

When it comes away it is called 'cleansing' and the ewe will often eat her own afterbirth. This is a natural instinct, as in the wild the bloody afterbirth would attract predators.

The first weeks

If a ewe has three lambs (treble), most farmers will take one of the lambs and adopt it on to a ewe with one lamb, as its own mother may have difficulty feeding three lambs as ewes only have two teats.

Persuading another ewe to feed a lamb that is not her own requires patience and persistence. The ewe must be held several times a day to allow the new lamb to suckle. Eventually her 'smell' will permeate the lamb through its drinking her milk and she will accept it as her own.

Inevitably some lambs are born dead, leaving a good milky ewe without a lamb. Some shepherds may skin the dead lamb and put the skin on a lamb which is to be adopted with the ewe. Because she thinks she can smell her own lamb (the skin) a ewe will nearly always take the new lamb straight away.

The first milk the ewe produces is called 'colostrum', which is very thick and contains antibodies which help to protect the lamb from disease. It is vital that all lambs get colostrum within the first few hours of birth. Some farmers will keep a stock of frozen

Housed ewes just lambed

colostrum for an emergency and commercial substitutes are available.

Sometimes a ewe may reject her own lamb or not have enough milk to feed it. If possible the shepherd will adopt the unwanted lamb with another ewe, otherwise it will be bottle-fed or put on an automatic feeder. Orphan lambs become very tame and will follow the person who feeds them.

In many flocks the lambs and mothers are numbered on their fleeces so it is easy to identify which lambs belong to which ewes.

Tame Lambs running to get a bottle

Most male lambs intended for meat are castrated with rubber rings soon after birth. The tails of most lambs are also ringed to make them drop off. This is done because if they get a blow-fly strike (flies laying their eggs which turn into maggots and eat the sheep alive) it is often in the tail which is soiled from the lambs own faces or urine. A short tail also makes shearing easier.

When the weather is good, ewes and lambs will be turned back out to grass within a day or two of the birth. By about four weeks, the lambs will begin to nibble grass and they may be fed concentrates. This is normally fed to lambs in a creep feeder which means the lambs can get through a gap to feed but not their dams (mothers).

In lowland flocks most lambs are finished (ready for slaughter) before they are weaned from the ewe although some may be weaned at around three to four months and finished on grass before being killed.

Lambs from upland flocks that come to the lowlands as store lambs will be finished later. They may be kept through the winter and fed on arable stubble, growing root crops such as turnips or kale, and some concentrates.

Kale (green crop) and turnips are usually 'strip grazed' by moving an electric fence over the field a few metres at a time, allowing the sheep to graze a thin strip of the crop at a time. This prevents over-eating and digestive problems such as bloat.

When the store lambs are heavy enough (36 to 46 kilograms live weight, probably between October and April) they will be sold at a market by auction, or moved directly to an abattoir. Ewes and lambs are brought into a fenced or yarded area quite regularly to be checked for health problems and to see if the lambs are suitable for market.

Pastures can carry high levels of parasite eggs such as gut worm, lungworm and liver fluke. These are ingested by animals and will affect their condition and performance. Unless they are farmed organically most sheep are dosed (drenched) on a regular basis to prevent the build-up of worms and liver fluke.

Particularly on lowland pasture, sheep's hooves (which grow like fingernails) need regular trimming to prevent infections like foot rot: in mountainous regions they are worn away naturally. Blow-fly can cause serious problems as well as sheep scab (mange) which causes the fleece to come away in clumps.

Many flocks are vaccinated against a range of diseases in the same way that we are. Recently

Ewe and lambs are numbered so the farmer knows which belong to which

a vaccine has been developed for a disease called Blue Tongue which is carried by midges and has crossed to the UK from Europe.

A race is used when handling large numbers of sheep. Races are normally made from small gates that inter-lock with each other to form a passageway from the collecting area to a handling pen which is the width of a sheep. The handling pen can be opened and shut from both ends allowing sheep to follow each other through it. Once the sheep are in a confined space it enables the shepherd to treat the animals. Some races are permanent structures and an automatic spray race can be used to control scab and blow-fly strike.

Sheep Dogs

A good working sheep dog is the shepherd's best friend and is as much part of the countryside now as it was 100 years ago.

Their keenness to round up sheep comes from the dogs' wish to gain their master's approval and to their natural hunting instinct, which has been controlled by training. The most common breed used as a sheep dog is the Border Collie although the Kelpie, Huntaway and the Bearded Collie are also used as working sheep dogs.

Shearing and Wool

Wool, which was once a mainstay of UK exports, has now become a by-product. Although we still export wool, the price paid to the farmer does not even cover the cost of shearing the sheep !

Much of the wool is used in carpet making, and artificial fibres have eaten into the clothing and carpet market. Unless a farmer keeps fewer than four sheep or is processing his own wool, the wool has to be sold through The British Wool Marketing Board, which sets the price and sells the wool in bales of eight or nine tons by auction on the open market, including online.

A few people have found alternative uses for their wool. One farmer is selling his as compost and a new company has been formed which buys the lowest value wool (coloured) for insulation.

Sheep are sheared in the early summer (and sometimes when they are housed in the

Weighing lambs

Sheep pens and race for easy handling

winter to stop them getting too hot.). Sheep fleeces are greasy because they contain lanolin which is secreted from the sheep's sebaceous glands to protect the fleece from rain and wind. Lanolin is extracted from the shorn fleece and is refined for many different uses, from medicinal to the lubricating of machine parts.

A few farmers may shear their own small flocks of sheep but most areas of Britain have local shearers who go to the same farms year after year. Because there are not enough British sheep shearers, most of the "clip" is carried out by gangs of shearers from Australia and New Zealand.

Keeping the fleeces clean is important during shearing, so a tarpaulin is spread out with a wooden board on top on which the sheep are shorn. Shearing a sheep is an exacting skill, although the practiced shearer can accomplish the task in under one minute. The shorn fleece is 'thrown' so it spreads out and can be folded in, then rolled tidily before being placed in a woolsack. The woolsack is hung on a frame so the fleeces can be tightly packed in. When it is full the sack is sewn up with string.

Mike Hallett shearing a sheep

Dairy Sheep

Sheep have been milked for thousands of years in Europe, and the British Sheep Dairying Association was formed in 1983 as more people became familiar with continental sheep cheeses such as Feta, Ricotta and Pecorino Romano. There was also a growing interest in the health giving properties of sheep milk.

Sheep milk is pure white and does not have a strong taste. The fats and proteins in sheep milk break down more readily in the human stomach than cow's milk, and it has almost double the amount of calcium. It is also packed full of protein, amino acids, vitamins and minerals. People who are allergic to cow's milk are often able to drink sheep milk and eat its products.

Ewes in milking stalls

The UK has some two hundred flocks of dairy sheep and they are milked in adapted milking parlours. Sheep have a lactation period of 180 to 210 days and a pure milking breed will give 450 to 550 litres over this period.

Although any sheep can be milked, the four most prominent commercial milking breeds are the Friesland, Colbred, Dorset and British Milksheep, or crosses with them. Economic flock sizes generally range from 250 to 500.

The main products are cheese with a smaller market for milk, yoghurt and ice-cream. All these breeds will also have a wool crop.

Sheep Breeds

Despite increased interest in ewes for dairying, most sheep reared in Britain today are raised for meat or breeding. Unlike cattle, where a few breeds dominate, many sheep breeds play an important role in meat production. The exception to this are the very rare breeds which have been preserved in small flocks, but while they are not commercially significant they provide a valuable role in conservation grazing and widen the genetic pool of the national sheep flock.

Where a breed is listed by the Rare Breeds Survival Trust, it is in *italics*.

Badger Face Welsh Mountain (1)

There are two distinctive varieties of the Badger Face: Torddu (Welsh for 'black belly) and Torwen (Welsh for 'white belly'). These are hardy sheep with compact and strong bodies and are farmed both as hill and lowland sheep. Usually the rams have horns and the ewes are polled.

Balwen Welsh Mountain (2)

The Balwen Welsh Mountain is one of the original breeds of Welsh Mountain sheep, from Cardigan, Brecon and Carmarthen. It was virtually wiped out in the harsh winter of 1947. Small and easy to manage the ewes are polled, the rams horned and they produce sweet tasting meat.

Beltex (3)

The Beltex (Belgian Texel) originates from Belgium and was introduced to the UK in 1989. The most prominent feature of the Beltex is their distinctive double-muscled hindquarter developed through selection and cross-breeding. The Beltex is primarily used as a terminal sire, producing good quality lambs for meat.

Berrichon Du Cher (4)

The Berrichon Du Cher originates from the Cher region of France. The sheep are polled, and are mostly used to produce meat out-of-season; the breed is notable for the fact that the ewes can lamb throughout the year, and can produce heavy and active lambs up to three times in two years.

Beulah Speckled Face (5)

The Beulah Speckled Face is mainly found in mid-Wales. The ewes are naturally polled and are known for their excellent maternal instincts and milking qualities. The breed is larger than the true mountain sheep, with the ewes being prized for cross-breeding on the lowlands, and producing good quality finished and store lambs.

Blackface (Scottish Blackface) (6)

This breed of sheep is one of the most abundant in the UK, with the majority of flocks situated in Scotland. The Blackface is always horned and they are excellent grazers in upland environments. These sheep are known for their versatility, adaptability and hardiness, the lambs for their exceptional meat quality, and the wool is often used in carpet making.

Black Welsh Mountain (7)

As a mountain breed the Black Welsh are robust, enduring and naturally more resilient to foot rot and fly strike than other less hardy breeds. They generally need no extra feeding and flourish on the tough upland grasses. The meat from this breed is lean and sweet, whilst the wool can be used either to create a hard-wearing and warm cloth or thick rugs.

Bleu du Maine (8)

Originating in Western France, the Bleu du Maine was first introduced to Britain in the late 1970s and is best known for its high levels of fertility and lambs which will suckle within moments of birth. The high fertility rates of the rams means that the Bleu du Maine is often crossed with other breeds, where their prolific nature seems to be passed down to the next generation.

Bluefaced Leicester (9)

Originally called the Dishly Leicester, then the Hexham Leicester, the antecedents of the Bluefaced Leicester that we know today were created through a breeding scheme fashioned by Robert Bakewell in the 1750s. The Bluefaced Leicester is the most used crossing sire in Britain. The progeny of any ewe crossed with a Bluefaced Leicester is called a mule.

Border Leicester (10)

Another descendent of Robert Bakewell's improvement scheme, the Border Leicester came about thanks to George and Matthew Culley (students of Robert Bakewell) who made it possible for the Dishly Leicester to be crossed with both Teeswater and Cheviot ewes. Today, easy lambing, quality fleece, milkiness, hardiness and early maturing spring lambs make this a common breed.

Boreray (11)

In the 1930s the inhabitants of Hirta, the main island of St Kilda, evacuated the island, killing all of their domestic animals. However, a wild replacement flock survived on the neighboring island of Boreray. A small number of Boreray have been taken off the island in recent years and the breed is currently described as 'critically endangered'. Boreray are small, short-tailed sheep with strikingly curling horns, and they are agile, skilled climbers.

Brecknock Hill Cheviot (12)

Introduced to Brecknockshire from Scotland about one hundred and twenty years ago, this breed has become well suited to the hills and mountains of Wales, and is a very hardy sheep. The Brecknockhill Cheviot are kept as pure flocks for breeding replacements as well as for crossing with other breeds such as native hill breeds, Suffolks and Leicesters. The Cheviot is used both for prime lamb and fleece.

British Milksheep (13)

The British Milksheep was developed in the 1970s and firmly established in 1980 to produce a prolific ewe with good milking ability. Rams are used to cross with other breeds to improve their lambing performance and milkiness. Flocks of British Milksheep are of course also used as milking flocks.

Cambridge (14)

Developed in 1964 at Cambridge University by crossing Finn Rams with a number of different native ewes deemed to be very prolific (such as Clun Forest, Llanwenog and Lleyn), the Cambridge is used primarily for breeding to produce excellent quality halfbred ewes. These ewes are then crossed with rams specifically to produce lamb for the modern meat market.

Castlemilk Moorit (15)

The Castlemilk Moorit were originally bred as an ornamental breed to grace the parklands of the Castlemilk estate in Scotland. In the 1970s there were just six ewes and a ram remaining of the breed, and all of the sheep we have today are descended from them. The meat is said to taste slightly gamey as they are slow to mature. The fleece is soft, short, even and tight and is cast-off in the summer rather than being shorn; it is often used in tweed making.

Charmoise Hill (16)

One of, if not the, earliest imported hill breeds to Britain, the Charmoise Hill was produced in France in the late 1700s by crossing native hill breeds with Kent Rams. One of the key uses of the Charmoise ram is in crossbreeding to produce quality lamb and for easy lambing. Ewes are maternal and milky and can lamb out-of-season if required.

Charollais (17)

The Charollais was introduced to Britain from France in the mid 1970s. Its popularity is growing by the year: it is one of the most numerous terminal sires in Britain. Rams are celebrated for their sexual activity and the quantity of lambs produced, whilst the size and shape of the breed ensures easy lambing.

Cheviot (18)

In 1372 a small and hardy sheep was thriving in the Cheviot Hills, on the border between Scotland and England. It is likely that these are the ancestors of the modern Cheviot. Although legend has it that during the Spanish Armada, some sheep swam to the English shore from a wrecked Spanish boat which is why the breed is known to have come 'up out of the sea'. Today the Cheviot is a larger sheep with a heavier fleece and its main use is for prime lamb. The wool of the Cheviot was formerly the base for the Border Tweed industry but it has declined in importance.

Clun Forest (19)

The Clun Forest sheep is known for its longevity, resistance to disease and low mortality rate. The main purpose of the breed is to produce hybrid ewes; it has been crossed with the Blue Faced Leicester and Border Leicester successfully for a number of years, and more recently with continental breeds to produce lamb suitable for modern tastes.

Colbred (20)

Named after Oscar Colborn of Gloucester-shire, the Colbred was developed by crossing Dorset Horns, Clun Forest, East Frieslands and Suffolks. Colborn's aim was to produce a sheep with better carcass quality, mothering ability and fertility. The Colbred has become one of the four main breeds of sheep in Britain to be used within dairy flocks (the others being the Friesland, British Milksheep and Dorset).

Cotswold (21)

It is believed that the Cotswold was introduced to Britain by the Romans in the first century A.D. The medieval wool churches in the Cotswolds bear testament to the importance of their fleece both locally and nationally. Named after the cots or cotes which were their shelters and the wold (wide open country), it has been argued that the Cotswold Hills were named after the sheep. This is a large breed with thick, coarse, wavy wool and mild flavoured meat.

Dalesbred (22)

The progeny of the Swaledale and Scottish Blackface, the Dalesbred is indigenous to the Yorkshire Dales. With is characteristic white markings above each nostril, and low round horns, the Dalesbred is used both for quality lamb, crossbreeding with Teeswater Rams to produce the Masham, fleece for carpets and tweeds, and as a draft ewe.

Dartmoor (Greyface) (23)

The Greyfaced Dartmoor is a robust, placid and easy to handle breed. The breed is descended from sheep which grazed in and around Dartmoor. Although slow to mature (they do not lamb until they are two years old) the meat is excellent. Both sexes are naturally polled medium-sized sheep. The fleece, classed as Lustre Longwool, is growing in popularity and is considered very good for rug making.

Derbyshire Gritstone (24)

Developed in the mid eighteenth century on the edge of the Peak District, the Derbyshire Gritstone was originally called the Dale O'Goyt, and is one of the oldest hill breeds in Britain. Both sexes are polled and the fleece produces excellent quality wool. This is a large breed, robust, hardy and well adapted to foraging for food in difficult environments.

Devon Closewool (25)

A docile breed of sheep originating on Exmoor, the Devon Closewool is predominantly a grassland sheep and is ideal for first time sheep keepers. It is naturally polled with a fine, close fleece which is ideal for home spinning. Lambs mature early and they are an economical and hardy breed that is easy to care for.

Devon and Cornwall Longwool (26)

In 1977 the South Devon Flock Book and the Devon Longwool Sheep Breeders Society amalgamated and created the Devon and Cornwall Longwool. The South Devon was a larger breed. The Devon Longwool was much smaller. The result is a large docile grassland sheep with a very strong and heavy fleece (the breed produces more wool than any other British sheep) used for carpets, rugs and tweed. Pure bred carcasses are lean with an excellent conformation and are extremely well flavoured.

Dorset Down (27)

In the first decade of the nineteenth century Southdown rams were crossed with Hampshire, Wiltshire and Berkshire ewes, producing a hardy, placid and adaptable breed with excellent mothering ability and easy lambing which in 1906 was officially established as the Dorset Down. The breed is one of the best for early maturing, making the Dorset Down excellent as a terminal sire.

Dorset Horn & Poll Dorset (28)

One of the earliest recorded breeds in Britain, and best known for their ability to lamb at any time during the year (sometimes lambing three times in two years), their adaptability to different environments, milkiness and prime carcasses. The first Dorset Horns were imported to Australia in 1895, where they were crossbred to produce the Dorset Poll. In the 1950s two Dorset Poll Rams were brought to Britain from Australia, and the Poll now far exceeds the Horn in numbers.

Est à Laine Merino (29)

The Est à Laine Merino developed from the original Merino being crossed with German sheep native to the French/German border. There were large numbers of them in the Alsace Lorraine area of France, and it was these sheep that became known as Est à Laine Merino. The breed is naturally polled and produces a fine white fleece, ideal for making felt. Ewes are prolific, milky and maternal, and are often crossed with meat breeds to produce good quality, fast-maturing lamb.

Exmoor Horn (30)

The Exmoor Horn is a sturdy and handsome hill breed with a white face and large curling horns, and a good quality fleece. Found mainly in the upland areas of the West country, particularly Devon, the Exmoor Horn ewe is often in demand by lowland breeders as a crossing ewe, producing good quality half-bred ewes which are prolific, hardy and have excellent lambs for the meat trade.

Friesland (31)

The Friesland is the only pure dairy breed in Britain. All breeds of sheep can of course give milk after they have lambed, but due to the Freisland's large body capacity they are able to have five to six lambs at a time (though two or three is more normal). This means the Freisland can produce much more milk than other breeds. Freislands are naturally polled with fine white fleeces and a long bald tail.

Galway (32)

The Galway was developed in the West of Ireland and said to be Ireland's only native breed. It was firstly known as the Roscommon sheep but in the 1920s became known as the Galway. It is a big hornless white sheep with a small top-knot of wool on the forehead. It is classed as a Longwool but the fine textured wool is of medium length. The breed is docile, long-lived and quite prolific.

Gotland (33)

Introduced to Britain in 1972 and again in 1984, the breed originates from the Swedish island of Gotland where it is said to have been established by Vikings. The Gotland is a polled, long woolled, short tailed sheep with a fleece of silvery grey. The furskin of the Gotland is highly prized, being soft and warm, though the breed is also kept for meat and fleece.

Hampshire Down (34)

The Hampshire Down was developed by crossing the Wiltshire Horn and Berkshire Knot with the Southdown. The breed was extremely important in the south of England, in particular Hampshire, Wiltshire and Berkshire, for keeping the light soils fertile. Usually easy to lamb, ewes have two or more lambs, are milky and maternal and would naturally lamb in December. The fleece is used in felts, hosiery and for hand-knitting wools.

Hebridean (35)

From the Western Isles of Scotland, the continuing existence of the breed is mostly due to the large estates and parklands in Scotland and England which, in the nineteenth century, began to house flocks of Hebridean sheep (mostly black in colour) for ornamental purposes. The native Hebridean sheep were all but extinct by the twentieth century. Due to the fact that the breed has not been extensively developed or modified by cross-breeding, the Hebridean sheep are hardy, small and economical. Hebrideans are slower to mature and their meat is lean and dark with a deep, gamey flavour.

Herdwick (36)

Due to the intense weather conditions of the central and western Lake District, the Herdwicks are extremely hardy with tough, wiry wool. Such wool is not easy to knit with, although with perseverance, one can create garments which repel the rain and last far longer than other woollen clothing. The word 'Herwick' (meaning sheep pasture) can be traced back to the twelfth century. Herdwick are known for their lifelong ability to remember where on the fell they belong. Today they are kept for carpet wool and meat.

Hill Radnor (37)

As with many of the hill or mountain breeds, the Hill Radnor is extremely thrifty, hardy, and good at foraging. The fleece is lighter in colour than many upland breeds, though dense, and as such is often in high demand from local weavers and hand-spinners. The Hill Radnor is mostly found on the borders of Wales and England

Icelandic (38)

This fine-boned, medium-sized and short-tailed breed is one of the oldest pure domesticated breeds in the world. Icelandic sheep are docile and can withstand poor grazing. The fleece is beautiful and double-coated, with a long outer coat (tog) and soft inner coat (thel). Because of the variety of colours (from black, through grey, apricot and fawn) and patterns of the fleece (speckled, striped and lined) it is well sought after by spinners and felters.

Jacob (39)

The distinctive mottled Jacob sheep is said to be named after the Genesis story in which Jacob becomes a shepherd of pied sheep. The earliest records of Jacobs being imported to Britain date to the 1750s, where a flock was established (for ornamental purposes) at Charlecote Park in Warwickshire which is still there today. They can have one or two pairs of horns, the meat is lean and sweet whilst their wool is good for spinning and weaving.

Kerry Hill (40)

Although listed as a rare breed for some time, the Kerry Hill has regained some popularity of late, perhaps due to its wonderful markings (which are particularly lovely on the lambs). The breed is named after the small town of Kerry, near Newtown in Powys. The fleece is soft and dense, and the Kerry Hill crosses well with hill and long wool breeds.

Leicester Longwool (41)

This breed originally comes from Leicester and the surrounding counties. In the 1700s the breed was 'improved' by Robert Bakewell, producing a sheep that was early to mature. Today the Leicester Longwool is a large hardy breed, naturally polled and with a lustrous and silky fleece. It is a good cross for upland ewes as it passes on the inherited traits of easy management, durability and early finishing.

Lincoln Longwool (42)

The Lincoln Longwool has similar origins to the Leicester Longwool. Robert Bakewell, the famous 'improver', first identified the old Lincoln, and subsequently Lincolnshire breeders used his new Leicester rams with old Lincoln ewes to eventually produce the sheep known today as the Lincoln Longwool. This improved breed produced more meat and wool per sheep.

Llanwenog (43)

In the late nineteenth century Shropshire Down sheep were introduced to the Teifi Valley in West Wales, and crossed with a now extinct local hill sheep (the Llanllwni). The resulting black faced and polled ewe inherited the favourable traits of both breeds: hardiness, milkiness, good conformation and perhaps most importantly, productiveness. The fleece is of great quality and is excellent for hand-spinning.

Lleyn (44)

Lleyn ewes are tremendous mothers: they seldom need feeding concentrates and are known for their longevity and resistance to disease. It is only recently that the breed, which is native to the Lleyn peninsular, has become popular outside of this beautiful pocket of Wales. Rams are used in cross-breeding to pass on maternal characteristics and prolificacy, and for producing prime lamb.

Lonk (45)

An extremely hardy, handsome horned sheep, the Lonk is one of the largest breeds native to the British Isles. From the Yorkshire and Lancashire Pennines, it has a long history in the area and was certainly one of the breeds farmed by Cistercian monks at both Sawley and Whalley Abbeys. Lonk ewes are good mothers, usually producing a single lamb. The breed is mainly used for meat and for wool in carpet making.

Manx Loghtan (46)

The Manx Loghtan is a short-tailed breed indigenous to the Isle of Man, although other flocks exist throughout the British Isles. The breed is unusual in that both ewes and rams have two or three pairs of horns. The fleece is brown with light tips and commonly left un-dyed and used to weave light-weight clothes, as well as Manx tartans. The meat of the breed is highly prized, and protected by EU law.

Masham (47)

The progeny of the Teeswater ram and either a Dalesbred, Swaledale or Blackfaced ewe, the Masham sheep has been bred predominantly in the northern counties of England for over a hundred years. The inherited qualities of the Masham include longevity, hardiness, milkiness and prolificacy.

Meatlinc (48)

The primary purpose for the development of this breed by Henry Fell in the 1960s was to produce quality rams (terminal sires) in order to yield robust, fast-growing lambs with pure or cross-bred ewes, specifically for the commercial meat market. One of the largest of the British breeds, the Meatlinc is economical and is also suited to a range of different environments.

Norfolk Horn (49)

The Norfolk Horn originates from the heathland of Norfolk. A popular sheep until the mid nineteenth century but by the 1960s only a handful of the breed remained. A breeding program was undertaken in the 1970s which has saved the breed from extinction, though it is still classified as a rare breed. The meat is lean and succulent and a little like venison.

North Country Cheviot (50)

In the eighteenth century, Sir John Sinclair took five hundred 'long hill sheep' from the Cheviot Hills to his home in Caithness in a bid to put a stop to the declining quality of Scottish and English sheep. The breed rapidly spread across Scotland. They are a large breed, adaptable, maternal, prolific and produce good quality lamb.

North of England Mule (51)

The progeny of Bluefaced Leicester rams and Swaledale ewes, the North of England Mule retains its mother's robust and maternal nature and its father's high fertility, and good sized carcass. Ram lambs are used as prime quality lamb, whilst ewes (or mules) are kept for crossing with other breeds such as the Suffolk and Texel to provide lambs for the meat market. Many believe that the North of England Mule is the UK's most important commercial sheep.

North Ronaldsay (52)

Most noted for its unusual diet of seaweed, the origins of the North Ronaldsay have been much debated. Some argue that the genetic material of the breed is similar to that of sheep living at the Neolithic site of Skara Brae, Orkney, three thousand years ago. The sheep adapted to a diet of mainly seaweed after a wall was built around the island in 1834, relegating them to the foreshore to protect inland grazing. The meat is lean and full of flavour, although lambs are slow to mature. Fleece can be a variety of colours and is popular for felting and hand spinning.

Oxford Down (53)

An extremely popular breed in the first half of the twentieth century, the Oxford Down was developed in the 1830s by crossing Hampshire Down and Southdown ewes with Cotswold rams. Originally used mainly for mutton and wool, the Oxford Down has enjoyed something of a come-back as a crossing sire, largely because the heavy and lean lambs mature early.

Portland (54)

One of the defining characteristics of this rare breed is that it was one of the first breeds of sheep to lamb at any time during the year, and usually only has a single lamb. The Portland is a comparatively small heathland sheep most commonly associated with the Isle of Portland, in Dorset. Both sexes have horns, the males heavily spiraled, and the lambs are born a delightful russet colour, changing to grey or white in the first few months.

Romney (55)

Named after the Romney Marsh in Kent, this breed was developed as a dual purpose sheep to produce both quality fleece and meat. The Romney is a large, hardy and versatile sheep which has good disease, worm and footrot resistance, with heavy, long and excellent quality wool. It has been exported and bred across the globe because of its ability to adapt to a range of climates and farming systems

Rouge De L'ouest (56)

The Rouge De L'ouest (Red of the West) is most commonly used as a terminal sire for market lamb production in Britain today. Originally from the Loire region of France, it was popular as a dairy breed for makers of camembert. The head of the Rouge De L'ouest is red or pink in colour. The breed is strong with a superior conformation in addition to prolificacy and milkiness.

Rough Fell (57)

The Rough Fell is a robust breed from the uplands of the north of England, common upon moorland and fell farms in Yorkshire, Cumbria and Lancashire. One of the largest mountain breeds in Britain, it is a docile animal which requires little maintenance. The fleece is used in Britain for carpeting, and is exported for making mattresses.

Roussin (58)

Imported to Britain in 1982, the Roussin is the offspring of the Brittany Heath sheep and British breeds such as the Southdown and Suffolk. The Roussin ram is used to sire cross bred females from hill breeds, passing on the positive attributes such as prolificacy and ease of lambing. The carcass has a good conformation and meets the needs of the meat market.

Ryeland (59)

Ryelands are ideal sheep for the smallholder or those new to sheep keeping due to their small to medium size (making handling them much easier) their fertility, good meat and economical nature. The forerunners of the modern Ryeland were developed in the fifteenth century by Herefordshire monks who grazed the sheep on areas of rye to enhance the rye yield. Ewes are extremely maternal and the wool is much sought after by hand spinners.

Romanov (60)

The name 'Romanov' comes from the former royal family of Russia and the sheep originated in the Volga Valley. They are now found throughout the world. The ewes are prolific, producing two to five lambs at a time. When they are born the lambs are jet black but as they get older the fleece turns grey. They are naturally a short tailed breed. Traditionally the wool is used for rugs, carpets and wall hangings and the meat is eaten.

Scotch Half Bred (61)

The Scotch Half Bred was created in the mid eighteenth century by crossing a Border Leicester ram with a North Country Cheviot Ewe. Also known as the 'Queen of Sheep' the Scotch Half Bred ewe is renowned for her fertility and ability to produce good quality lambs. Ewe lambs are used for breeding and are crossed with breeds such as the Suffolk to provide early lamb for the spring market.

Scotch Mule (62)

The term 'mule', when applied to a sheep, means that it has been sired by a Blue Faced Leicester. Mules are the most numerous of sheep in the UK used for commercial purposes and the Scotch Mule, being the progeny of the Blue Faced Leicester crossed with a Blackface ewe, is the most popular. The Blue Faced Leicester ram transfers many attractive qualities to the Scotch Mule, including higher milk yield and early maturity of lambs.

Scottish Blackface (see Blackface)

Scottish Greyface (63)

The Scottish Greyface was almost certainly being bred in Scotland by 1870, when Border Leicester rams were being crossed with Blackfaced ewes. Greyface ewes are often sold to lowland breeders in order to produce lambs with a prime carcass which are early to mature. Her body is long, lean and even, and can be found in most parts of the UK, although the breed is less common in other parts of the world.

Shetland (64)

The Shetland is an unimproved northern short-tailed sheep. The Shetland is a small and hardy sheep, adaptable to a variety of environments. Perhaps the most notable feature of the breed is the variety of its fleece colour and markings. There are eleven primary fleece colours with thirty different types of marking known. The fleece, being soft and of a high quality, is excellent for hand spinners and is still highly prized.

Shetland-Cheviot (65)

The Shetland-Cheviot is produced by crossing a Shetland ewe with a North County Cheviot ram. The breed was developed at the beginning of the twentieth century to produce prime lamb. The Shetland-Cheviot inherits the positive characteristics from each parent: the hardiness and milkiness of the ewe and the good conformation of the ram. It has a fine white fleece which is used for knitwear and tweed.

Shropshire (66)

The exact origins of the modern Shropshire breed are slightly hazy. It is thought that sheep native to the counties of Shropshire and Staffordshire were crossed first with the Southdown and later, to produce a more docile sheep, the Leicester. A medium-sized sheep, the Shropshire is covered with a dense fleece and is one of the heaviest wool producers of its size. The breed is gentle and docile, naturally polled with a black face and white fleece.

Soay (67)

Originally from the Island of Soay in the St Kilder group, the breed has been described as an example of the types of sheep that would have been kept by people in the Bronze Age. The Soay is a small, fine boned sheep with chocolate or tan coloured fleece which is normally shed in the spring. Soay are happy grazing in the uplands, in woodland or lowland pastures. Ewes are extremely maternal, the meat is known for its leanness and distinctive flavour whilst the wool is used for specialty yarns.

Southdown (68)

Purported to be one of our oldest breeds, the Southdown hales from the Sussex area in southeast England. Due to the excellent conformation and the high quality of the meat, it has been used extensively in the improvement of many other breeds. The Southdown is docile and easy to handle, is excellent as a crossing sire and has a medium length fine grade fleece.

South Wales Mountain (69)

Believed to derive from the same stock as the Welsh Mountain breed, the South Wales Mountain sheep graces the upland areas of Carmarthenshire, Powys, Glamorgan and Monmouthshire. It is larger than other Welsh Mountain breeds and has a unique brown collar and tan markings on its legs and face. Living in the Welsh uplands in often harsh weather conditions, the breed has a dense and weather-proof fleece and is extremely hardy.

Suffolk (70)

The Suffolk sheep is one of the leading terminal sires in the UK and there are records of the breed dating back to the late 1790s. The Suffolk was developed by crossing Norfolk Horn ewes with Southdown rams and at the time the resultant sheep were known as 'blackfaces' or 'Southdown Norfolks'. A strong and sturdy breed, the Suffolk is also full of character and is a favourite worldwide for producing excellent quality lamb.

Swaledale (71)

Originally from the upland areas of the northern counties of England, particularly Yorkshire, the Swaledale is now found throughout the country and has proved itself to be adaptable to lowland areas. A hardy sheep, the Swaledale is horned and known for its off-white fleece. It produces good quality and tasty meat and provides excellent mutton.

Teeswater (72)

The Teeswater is a longwool sheep which evolved near the River Tees in the Peninnes, northern England. However, the breed lost popularity during the nineteenth century, and despite a revival of interest the breed is still classed as vulnerable by the Rare Breeds Survival Trust. The Teeswater has exceptional quality wool is used as a sire with many horned sheep breeds.

Texel (73)

The most dominant terminal sire breed in Europe, the Texel is originally from the Island of Texel off the coast of The Netherlands. The first Texel rams were brought to Britain in the early 1970s, and soon more ewes and rams followed. In the ensuing forty years the British Texel has proved its adaptability to both lowland and upland environments whilst the carcass is both lean and of a high quality.

Vendeen (74)

Tales of sheep rescued from wrecks of Spanish galleons during the Armarda accompany the history of this breed, but unfortunately there is no evidence to substantiate such claims. What we do know, however, is that Southdown Rams were introduced to the Vendee region of France and the modern breed developed from the offspring of these rams with local ewes. Vendeen sheep came to Britain in 1981, are comparatively docile and therefore easy to manage, and are principally used for the production of prime lamb.

Welsh Half-Bred (75)

The Welsh Half-bred is the progeny of a Welsh Mountain ewe and a Border Leicester Ram. Welsh Half-bred ewes are maternal, hardy, prolific and good milkers. Ewes are crossed with a terminal sire from breeds such as a Suffolk or Charollais in order to produce fast-growing lambs which have a lean carcass.

Welsh Hill Speckled Face (76)

Slightly larger than the Welsh Mountain sheep, the Welsh Hill Speckled Face is another of the breeds well-suited to living on some of the highest grounds in Britain. Developed in and around the Devil's Bridge area of mid Wales, the breed is characterized by black markings around the eyes and mouth, the knees of the front legs and all four feet. Purebred ewes make excellent mothers and are adaptable to both lowland and highland environments.

Welsh Mountain (77)
(Hill Flock or Registered)

The white Welsh Mountain sheep is small and hardy. Living in the higher parts of the Welsh mountains, it is also the most numerous of the various Welsh Mountain breeds. Due to the often cold and wet environment that the breed inhabits, it has been developed to enhance milkiness, mothering ability and lambs which are quick to suckle

Welsh Mule (78)

The primary purpose of the Welsh Mule is to produce fine quality lambs for the modern meat market. The breed was developed in the 1970s by crossing a Bluefaced Leicester with one of the three primary Welsh hill breeds (Welsh Mountain, Beulah or Welsh Hill Speckled Face), yielding ewes with their positive characteristics such as good foraging abilities, excellent mothering and hardiness.

Wensleydale (79)

One of the heaviest of our native breeds, the Wensleydale was created in North Yorkshire in the nineteenth century by crossing a single ram (named Bluecap) with a local long wool breed. The Wensleydale is used both as a crossing sire with hill ewes to produce productive breeding ewes and for its fleece. The wool of the Wensleydale is globally renowned for its excellence and lustrousness, and the ram of the breed is used as a wool improver worldwide.

intelligent, affectionate and full of fun; you have to think one step ahead of them to avoid escapees who would follow you back home.

The goat is a seasonal breeder under natural light conditions and would normally mate in the autumn. But to ensure an all year round milk supply, artificial lighting and hormones may be used to bring the doe into oestrus.

Normally the male goat will run with the females; the billy goat has a strong smell about him particularly in the breeding season. Artificial Insemination is sometimes used for goat production.

British Saanen goat kids

Encouraging kids to get up

The gestation period is about five months and from one to five kids can be born: most commonly it is two. Most does kid easily and are good mothers.

In dairy herds the kids are removed from their mother after two days when they have drunk colostrum, the first milk that is essential for the kid's wellbeing. They will be reared on formula milk, and the females kept as milking herd replacements.

If there is a market, male offspring will be castrated with a rubber ring (elastrator) and be reared for meat on farm or sold to a meat producer. Sadly most male kids are humanely destroyed at birth as there is not a significant UK market for goat meat, except for halal.

Most dairy goat kids are disbudded (horn buds are removed) in the first week of life. An anaesthetic is injected and a red hot iron with an open end pricks out the horn bud and cauterises the wound. In the UK this can only be done by a veterinary surgeon.

As with other livestock, it is a legal requirement for all goats to be ear tagged with a herd number, and a unique individual identification number.

Goats' hooves are susceptible to foot rot and need regular trimming with foot shears. This does not hurt the goat as the excess hoof can be trimmed like finger nails. Goats also suffer badly from intestinal worms and need regular worming.

Commercially there are only around fifty milking herds in the UK with an average of nine hundred goats; they only produce thirty five percent of the fifty million litres of milk needed for the liquid goat milk market, for cheese, and for yoghurt. The rest is imported from other European countries.

Many smallholders keep a few milking goats to produce milk and meat for their own consumption; it is now illegal to sell milk to the general public unless you are a Licensed Dairy Premises.

Because of EU legislation, many smaller producers of goats' milk were forced out of business. There are no quotas on goats' milk as there are on cows. Goats are very efficient converters of food and when compared kilogram for kilogram they produce more milk than cows.

The most common pure breeds used for dairying are British Saanen, Anglo Nubian, British Toggenburg and British Alpine but many goats in commercial herds are British Saanen crosses.

Goats' milk has smaller fat globules, which makes it more digestible and it has lower cholesterol levels than cow's milk. Many people who are allergic to cow's milk can drink goat's milk which is also valued for children with eczema and asthma.

Goats' milk looks whiter than cows' milk and if the milking practice is correct it has no taint despite a common belief to the contrary.

Commercially they are milked in adapted milking parlours in the same way as cows; more goats are milked at one time than cows and they milk more quickly. A goat will give an average yield of nine hundred litres per lactation.

In the milking parlour

A doe will milk commercially for about six lactations and much longer as a house goat; their natural life span is around fifteen years but they can live longer if well cared for. Does will also milk for two lactations without being put in kid again although the milk yield drops off in the second year.

After their useful life as a commercial dairy goat they are usually sent to market. If they are lucky they will be bought as

Housed dairy goats

Goats make good companions

Angora billy goat

Skins from all breeds of goats are used as rugs, for clothing, bags, shoes and drum skins.

Angora goats are also kept for their fibre called mohair, one of the warmest natural fibres, and cashmere comes mainly from Pashmina goats.

Angoras are the only breed of goat to have a single coat of hair; all other goat breeds are double-coated: they have a fine downy under coat and coarse outer coat of guard hairs. Mohair is obtained by shearing the Angora goats, usually twice a year. Cashmere is either combed from the goat during the spring moult or sometimes by shearing the animal.

Since the goat was first domesticated it has been used as a beast of burden and still is in many countries. In the UK there is a Harness Goat Society which promotes the use of working goats of all breeds. They may be seen at country shows pulling small carts either in pairs or by one animal.

companion animals or as house goats, but most will go for slaughter and be taken up for the halal meat trade where the meat is more appreciated.

In the last decade or so some British farmers have begun specialising in goat meat production, mainly from Boer goats and their crosses. Boer goats originated in South Africa and were specifically developed for their meat qualities.

When they kid does are kept indoors, away from predators. Then the goats will be grazed for as much of the year as possible with access to shelters. The meat used is from young animals between four and twelve months old.

Generally the marketing of the meat is directly from the farms or through farmers markets or via mail order.

Goat meat is considered to be very healthy; it is low in cholesterol and high in iron and has less saturated fat than chicken. It is succulent and sweet, very much like lamb without the greasiness, and with a hint of game in it.

Shearing an Angora goat

Goat breeds

Anglo Nubian

The Anglo Nubian is one of the largest and tallest breeds of goat; males can weigh up to one hundred and forty kilograms. It has a regal bearing, very distinctive head with a Roman nose and long pendulous ears. Their coat can be one colour or numerous colour combinations with a mottled effect, ranging right through black, brown, fawn, cream and white. They are used for their milk, which has a high butterfat and protein content and for their meat.

Saanen and British Saanen

There are limited numbers of pure Saanens in the UK. They originate from the Saanen valley in Switzerland where they are used as dairy goats. The British Saanen goat is larger than the Swiss Saanen which was imported into the UK from Holland in 1922 and from which the British Saanen developed. Like the Swiss goat it has a short fine white coat and a very friendly disposition. They have a high milk yield with a long lactation, so are the preferred breed for commercial dairy producers. They are often crossed with other breeds to improve the milk output.

British Alpine

This goat was first recognised in England in the early 1900s and they are thought to have resulted from the import of a black female goat from a Paris zoo. She was mated with an imported Toggenburg goat and their offspring carried the black colour.

They are black and white with distinctive markings which are referred to as being 'Swiss'. The black coat is short and shiny and framed by a white striped face, and white inner ears, tail, lower legs and white around the udder and rump. It is a good milking goat which will milk for a second year without having to kid. A good browser, it has a mischievous nature.

Anglo Nubian

British Saanen

British Alpine

Bantam Light Sussex

Araucana

Golden Silkie

The internet has provided another market for all kinds of hatching eggs which are auctioned and sent by post to the highest bidder. (Eggs do not have to be incubated immediately they are laid.)

Eggs are laid one at a time, and it is only when a clutch of 12 to 15 eggs have been laid that the hen sits on them to incubate the eggs. This ensures they will all develop at the same rate and hatch at the same time.

Commercial poultry farming in the UK is divided into two categories: laying hens for egg production and meat birds for eating, commonly known as 'broilers'. All large commercial flocks of fowl (including ducks and turkeys) are kept in housing with controlled lighting, temperature and ventilation and automatic feeders, drinkers and egg collection for layers. The housing is cleaned and disinfected between flocks.

Laying Hens

In the 1930s around one third of our eggs were imported as Britain's laying flocks were very small and kept to make 'pin' money for the farmer's wife. Birds were housed in a static shed with field access or in wooden field arcs that had to be moved to fresh grass by hand each day (chickens soon scratch up the grass in a small area).

In the 1940s many flocks were moved to a deep litter system where the birds were kept in large houses with perching areas and nest boxes, to which clean bedding in the form of straw or wood shavings, was added each day.

This raised bedding became fermented and provided compost over a period of time, which could then be spread on the fields as fertilizer.

Some farmers kept their chickens in houses with raised floors of wooden slats or wire mesh so the faeces dropped through and could be mucked out by hand.

As stocking rates increased, feather-pecking became more common and so did parasites such as Red Mites (which feed on chickens' blood whilst they are perching at night). These problems led to British farmers looking at the American system of keeping birds in cages.

Blue Orpington

Most of the traditional breeds of laying hens were removed from commercial use and hybrids based on White Leghorns, which laid white eggs, were used until the public demanded brown eggs.

Brown egg laying hybrids of the Rhode Island Red and the American New Hampshire took over.

The colour of the shell has nothing to do with the colour of the egg yolk, which is dictated by what the hen eats and there is no nutritional difference between brown and white shelled eggs.

Maran

In some indoor commercial production, colourants are added to the feed to make the yolk darker. Birds which roam freely can acquire some colourant through the colour of the different herbs and grasses they eat.

Tiered cages were introduced and the houses were windowless as it was realised that hens would lay more eggs if the light was controlled to provide a constant "summer." Without artificial light, pre-hybrid hens tended to lay from March to September. Insulation and ventilation systems were installed to control the temperature so now commercial hens lay all year round.

We consume around thirty million eggs per day in the UK, and there are now three main systems used for commercially producing eggs: enriched cages, barns and free-range.

Light Sussex

The most common hybrid breeds used for large-scale egg production in the UK are Isa Warren, Isa Brown, Shaver Brown, Lohmann, Columbian Blacktail and Hisex Brown.

All commercial laying chickens are hatched in huge industrial incubators. The day old chicks are sexed by hand on a production line. Only the female chicks are kept.

The male chicks, about fifty per cent of those hatched, do not put on weight quickly enough for meat production, and are killed. So are weak chicks. They are either gassed or macerated in a shredding machine. This is known as 'hatchery waste' and some may go to feed raptors.

The female chicks are reared by specialist units or sometimes by the egg producer. Most birds are vaccinated against salmonella and other diseases.

At sixteen weeks the birds are called pullets. They start laying eggs at between eighteen to twenty two weeks old. The farmer will encourage the hens to lay eggs in the nest boxes as eggs laid on the floor have to be collected by hand, will get dirty and not be

Golden Orpington

fit for human consumption. All eggs are stamped with a unique flock number for traceability.

In all intensive systems hens have a useful life of around thirteen months before their egg production drops away and they are slaughtered and replaced with a new batch of pullets. These are known as 'spent birds' and as they are mature will have a fuller flavour and darker meat which is not favoured by the UK consumer.

Spent birds are caught by teams of 'catchers' in low light conditions in order to cause the least amount of stress possible and to make the job easier, as hens cannot see to move in the dark. They are loaded into crates to be transported by lorry for slaughter and are often exported.

All poultry, which are omnivores, are fed on a mixed diet that is milled and supplied by

Silver Spangled Hamburgs

either the farm or specialist feed companies. Diets are usually entirely vegetarian with added vitamins, selenium and phosphate. They cannot contain meat and bone meal. Commercial egg producers have the feed blown into silos from which it is automatically distributed into the chicken sheds. Small flock keepers may purchase their feed in sacks.

Limestone provides calcium which is essential for forming egg shells. On a daily basis a laying hen will store reserves of calcium on her keel bone (medullary bone) and then draw it back down to form the egg shell over a twenty-three hour period.

Today's hens lay twice the number of eggs (about 300 per year) that they did in the 1930s. One hen will eat an average 125 grams of food per day.

Cages

Enriched laying cages (sometimes still known as Battery Cages), which are the most intensive method, are still the most common form of commercial egg production in the UK, providing about sixty per cent of the eggs that we eat. The cages must have a

Caged chickens before enriched cages

nesting and a scratching area and somewhere to perch. There can be many thousands of birds in one house.

Laying hens are usually de-beaked as chicks: the tip of the beak is removed to prevent them harming each other but still allow them to eat. Birds in cage systems are also prone to brittle bones and fractures.

Barn

In this system the hens are able to move around freely and stocking densities should be no more than nine birds per square metre of floor space.

Litter is provided for scratching and dust bathing, and perches must allow at least fifteen square centimetres of space per hen. Hens use communal nest boxes and the eggs drop onto a conveyor belt which takes them to a collection point.

Barn hens may be kept in flocks as small as five hundred, but units containing many thousands of birds must be divided into colonies of no more than four thousand.

Free Range

Free range flocks must have continuous day time access to vegetation, and stocking rates must not exceed 2,500 hens per hectare, although UK flocks are almost all stocked at significantly lower levels. Ranging areas can be protected by electric fencing to deter predators.

The laying sheds have exits known as 'pop-holes' which are opened each morning and closed in the evenings when the hens go back inside to roost. All hens need to be inside the house at some time in the day in order to lay their eggs.

Hens' access to range freely allows them to express their natural behavioural instincts by dust-bathing and to vary their diet by scratching for worms and eating vegetation.

There are some potential problems with free range systems as the hens are exposed to extremes of climate, parasites (worms) and have contact with wild birds, which might lead to avian flu. They are also vulnerable to foxes, or sudden stress from aircraft or hot air balloons.

Free range flocks vary from around 350 birds to many thousands in one house, Some free range birds may never leave their hen houses at all, either because there are not enough pop holes to get out, because they are unaware

Laying house

Racing out of the pop holes in the snow

they exist, or because they do not feel the need to leave.

The birds that do go outside generally stay close to the house unless there is tree cover, or purposely erected shaded areas. This may be because of fear of predators or due to their natural flocking instinct. Chickens don't like rain or very bright sunlight, and will seek cover, usually back inside the house, to avoid it.

As with other systems the flock will be culled when they have reached the end of their economic life.

Organic

Organic egg production is always free range and the land the chickens range on must be classed as organic (free from chemical fertilisers, pesticides and herbicides for at least two years).

Their feed has to be 100% organic, and stocking rates are considerably lower than those for conventional free range hens.

Packaging

Some larger egg producers are also packagers and will grade their eggs by size, date stamp them and sell them to supermarkets and wholesalers. They may also remove the shell and process the eggs ready for the catering, sandwich or manufacturing industries.

The majority of smaller commercial egg producers put their eggs in trays of thirty, stack them in six layers and then put them on pallets. Lorries transport the eggs to a packing station for grading, putting in cartons, processing and further distribution.

Smallholders mainly supply local outlets or sell their eggs direct from the farm gate or at farmers markets.

Automatically putting 30 eggs into a tray

Broiler chickens

'Broilers' are the chickens that are used for meat production and were introduced from America. They have been bred to gain weight very quickly so they can be slaughtered at a young age and still be tender. Male and female birds are reared.

Before the 1950s most poultry meat came from dual-purpose chickens that were kept for meat and eggs. In fact, poultry meat was considered a luxury and only eaten on special occasions.

Young broilers

Broilers are hatched from their parents, called broiler breeders, whose diet will be similar to laying hens, although the quantity is restricted to prevent the birds from becoming fat.

Broiler breeders produce approximately 135 chicks during their lifetime, which is around ten months. The eggs are hatched in incubators.

Day old chicks from the broiler breeders are moved to brooding areas in the sheds where they will spend the rest of their lives; there may be 25,000 or more in each shed.

As the broiler chicks grow they take up more space and they reach their killing weight of about two kilos in forty three days. Their diet is high in protein and energy and they have very little exercise.

This can cause problems: sitting on the litter for long periods can result in hock burns, breast blisters and weak legs. When they are ready to be killed, teams of catchers load the birds into crates to be transported for slaughter.

The majority of meat chickens in the UK are reared in this way.

Turkeys

Native to North America, wild Turkeys (*Meleagris Gallopauo*) roam in open woodland, roost in trees and have a life span of ten years or so.

Once a Christmas treat, twenty million turkeys are produced annually to supply what is now a year-round meat market.

Parent flocks are kept for breeding to supply eggs which are incubated and hatch after twenty seven days.

Turkeys have been selectively bred to produce large amounts of breast-meat.

Because of the large size of male turkeys (stags) they are often unable to mate naturally so artificial insemination is practised. The day old turkey chicks or poults (young birds) are transported in temperature controlled vehicles to the rearing farms. All newly hatched chicks have a residue of yolk inside their abdomens which provide them with food so they do not need to eat for up to two days once they hatch.

Straw or wood shavings are used to litter the floor. The very young birds have heat lamps to keep them warm.

Barn reared turkeys

The birds are fed on cereal based diets with added vitamins and sometimes fishmeal. Turkeys are vaccinated against a range of diseases and a wormer may be added to the feed. Antibiotic and hormonal growth promoters are not used in the UK.

Young birds do not fill the space and a shed may hold ten thousand, but as they grow so quickly they reach killing weights of 13 kilos in fourteen to twenty weeks. This can leave the birds packed closely together towards the end of their lives and they may have to be 'thinned out' to allow more floor space. The lighting is kept quite dim and the birds are often de-beaked to avoid them fighting and damaging each other.

Putting on weight so quickly, and the lack of exercise, means that the turkeys' legs may be unable to support their bodies..

Another less intensive way to rear turkeys is in pole barns which are more open to the elements. Partially open sides allow natural light and ventilation. The top half up to the roof is fenced with netting to stop wild birds entering.

Free range turkeys are stocked at lower densities still, and must have daylight access to vegetation. Predator proof fencing is essential around the whole range.

Two turkeys: a Norfolk Black and a Bronze

Guinea Fowl

Guinea fowl (*Numida Meleagris*) are native to West Africa where they forage for food in large flocks. The Portuguese introduced the birds into Europe in the sixteenth century and they have had a place on the British table since Elizabethan times.

They are related to chickens and partridge, but are classified as poultry and not game so cannot be hung to enhance the flavour. Guinea fowl are also known as Gleanies as they used to be turned out onto stubble fields to glean the dropped corn. Young Guinea Fowl are called keets.

Free range guinea fowl

There is only one large intensive supplier in the UK although smaller free range producers may supply a local market. Guinea Fowl is considered a delicacy but most guinea fowl eaten in the UK is imported in frozen form from elsewhere in Europe.

The distinctive feathers of the bird can be sold for making fishing flies and occasionally jewellery.

They lay their cone shaped eggs from spring to late autumn and the eggs take twenty eight days to hatch. The birds make good watch dogs and call loudly if a stranger or predator is around.

Guinea Fowl are not as disease-prone as other poultry and pick up much of their food in the form of insects if they have enough space to range. They need to be encouraged to go into a house at night otherwise they will roost in the trees and lay their eggs where they can't be found.

Quail

Japanese quail (*Coturnix Japonica*) have been bred in the Far East since the eleventh century. The French consume 250 million birds a year.

The UK is mainly a gourmet market of two to three million eating birds per year, with egg sales at around 175,000 eggs per week. A quail can lay two hundred and forty eggs per year and a meat bird has a live weight of approximately 230 grams.

Until fairly recently most quail production was in cages in intensive units. Public opinion has caused a move to aviary systems where the birds have outside access. They are delicate birds and have to be driven inside at night to avoid death due to exposure. For all-

Quail and eggs

year-round egg production lighting must be provided for sixteen hours a day when they are inside.

The quail are ready for slaughter at five to seven weeks of age and the major producers hatch, rear, process and distribute the birds from one site. Smaller producers will supply a local niche market.

Ducks

There are only a handful of large commercial producers of duck meat in the UK which between them produce about eighteen million birds a year. Demand for duck meat has risen in recent years, with much of it being used in restaurants: many Chinese dishes include duck meat.

Ducklings reach their live killing weight of around three and a half kilos at an age of forty nine days.

Free range commercial Aylesbury ducks

The most common breed used in commercial flocks is a cross between a Pekin and an Aylesbury duck. Other breeds for meat are Gressingham and Rouen. Breeding flocks and ducklings are reared in the same way as meat broilers.

Large producers have always claimed that providing ducks with access to water for bathing and preening would increase the possibility of water born disease (ducks both drink and evacuate into the water.)

If ducks are only able to drink from nipple drinkers they are unable to keep themselves clean and are subject to eye problems or even blindness.

Once again, public opinion has caused a move to free range rearing. In large free range systems a plastic flushing pond is supplied

Indian runners

Hen with ducklings she hatched

which can be cleaned and refilled regularly to minimise the risk of disease as ducks are relatively messy.

Khaki Campbell and Indian Runner ducks are kept for egg production. Duck eggs are not widely eaten in the UK as some people believe them, wrongly, to be strong-tasting or dirty. But eggs do sell to a niche market.

Geese

The goose was once the most common domesticated bird in Britain. They were kept to provide feathers for the arrows of longbows and for quills. Such was the demand for goose flight feathers that goose meat was once cheap and eaten by everyone.

Pilgrim goslings

Tolouse geese

The goose has now become more popular as a festive meal. Traditionally geese were fattened and driven to market by the farmer. This practice is still reflected in the names of fairs such as Nottingham and Tavistock Goose Fairs. The geese often travelled several miles and were 'shod' to protect their webbed feet.

Geese are grazing birds and they can be stocked at a rate of around 120 birds per hectare and usually cereal feed is made available. Geese must be housed at night to protect them from foxes.

Clean drinking and preening water should be available. Although geese can be reared intensively in sheds, it is not common practice in the UK as geese graze grass, which keeps rearing costs to a minimum.

Day old goslings require heat to survive so are kept in "brooders" with round-the-clock artificial light so they eat well and grow quickly until they are old enough to graze at about four weeks.

They are killed at around six months: the ganders (male birds) are heavier, weighing in at fourteen to fifteen kilos depending on the breed.

Large numbers are usually plucked with a dry plucking machine, although hand plucking is still in practice. The down (soft undercoat of feathers) from geese can be used for pillows and duvets.

Geese mate for life and breeding birds should be reared with each other, preferably from a day old, as they form strong bonds. It is usual to have one gander with three or four geese and they stay together. If unknown birds are introduced, they will fight them or try to drive them away.

A goose will lay eggs for ten or more years, producing thirty five to eighty eggs a year. They are protective parents.

The most popular breeds are Embden, Toulose, Roman, Pilgrim and Chinese.

Embden geese

Other Livestock

In recent years, with reduced farm incomes, the call for more exotic foods, and the rise of the farmers market, some farmers have moved into specialist areas. They involve some animals that may have only been viewed at zoos in the past.

Ostrich

To rear ostrich, a licence has to be obtained under the Dangerous Wild Animals Act. This can cost up to four hundred pounds each year and regular welfare and safety inspections are also costly.

There are around one hundred ostrich producers in the UK. The birds are kept for their meat, leather, and feathers and for breeding. The most common breed kept is the African Black. Ostriches are a grazing bird which do not need large amounts of land,

Ostrich with her eggs

although sturdy two-metre fencing is a must. Their diet is supplemented with cereal pellets.

They adapt easily to the British climate providing they have shelter from the wind and rain as their feathers contain little or no natural oil for protection. The females start egg production at around two years and they can often lay eggs for thirty years.

A female can lay 40 eggs in one year and the incubation period is 42-45 days: around half of the incubated eggs will be viable. When the young birds reach approximately 100 kilograms at around one year old, they will be slaughtered and provide a meat yield of some thirty kilograms. The meat is low in cholesterol and high in protein.

Wild Boar

The Wild Boar (Sus Scrofa) is common in Europe where it is hunted for sport and for its meat. It was once native to the UK but became extinct in the seventeenth century. It is now farmed to fill the market for exotic meat and breeding stock.

The boar can be farmed extensively (free range) or intensively, though both methods require a licence under the Dangerous Wild Animals Act.

There are around 2000 pure wild boar sows on British farms and a breeding group may contain five to twenty sows and one mature male. The average litter per year for a sow is around seven piglets. They are often crossed with a domestic breed which results in a 'hybrid' that increases the number of piglets in each litter.

Hybrid meat is paler and less flavoursome than pure wild boar meat which has a venison-red colour and a much more gamey taste. The meat is sold fresh or frozen especially at farmers markets and some is exported to France. It is processed into pates, terrines, hams and sausages.

Free range systems are preferable for wild boar as they mirror their natural environment of woodland and good ground cover, which in turn produces top quality meat. This means they can be reared on marginal land that is of little use for other agricultural activities. Shelters and farrowing arks should be provided and good fencing is essential.

In the wild their diet consists of vegetable material, fruit and small animals. Farmed boar should have vegetables in their diet and they also need a ration of cereal-based feed.

Intensive systems keep the wild boar indoors with a run-out, and divided pens for farrowing. The sow is one year old when she gives birth to her first boarlets and spring is the favoured time.

The gestation period is three months, three weeks and three days. The boarlets are weaned at eight to twelve weeks and given supplementary concentrated feed and vegetables. Slaughter weight of around eighty kilograms is reached when the animals are nine to twelve months old. The meat from older sows, even up to eight years, still has a commercial value and is perfectly palatable.

Buffalo

Water buffalo are descended from the Arni or Indian wild buffalo and have been domesticated for over four thousand years. Although they are classed as cattle in the UK they are unable to interbreed with cattle.

Despite their large size they are extremely docile and gentle, leading them to be worked by children in many parts of the world.

Buffalo are traditionally a triple purpose animal used for their milk, meat and for their pulling power. They are tolerant of the British weather and their husbandry is very similar to that of cattle: they can be kept in a loose yard, in cubicles and put to graze with good fences.

Buffalo have fewer sweat glands than other cattle and wallow in mud in their natural habitat to keep cool. In the UK, provided they have shade, they don't need to wallow. They are not generally dehorned as their horns are full of blood vessels which also act as a way of losing body heat.

Buffalo require a much lower intake of food than cattle and prefer shorter grass, so stocking density can be higher. Buffalo breed throughout the year and artificial insemination is not normally practised. The gestation period is around ten months with few calving difficulties as the calves are small. One calf is born each year.

Buffalo cows, which can milk for up to twenty years, are milked in a conventional milking parlour but they need practice to get used to it. They do not give as much milk as a dairy cow.

Wild boar ranging in scrubland

Buffalo waiting to be milked

Buffalo milk in not subject to EU Milk Quota, but all milking premises must be licensed, and all movements of animals have to be registered. Each animal must have a unique identity number.

Their sweet, pure white milk has a smooth creamy texture and is high in solids, making it ideal for processing into mozzarella, yoghurt, ice cream and mature cheeses. People who are allergic to cows' milk may be able to drink buffalo milk.

The meat contains half the fat of beef and is low in cholesterol.   Buffalo have not contracted BSE in any part of the world.

They are slaughtered from twenty four to thirty months when the animal weighs around five hundred kilograms. The killing-out percentage of meat is lower than that of cattle due to a heavier hide and head but this is offset by the price that buffalo meat commands.

Alpaca

Alpacas are domesticated members of the camelid family and come from South America. Many Alpaca owners are concentrating on breeding projects with the best animals to improve and expand the UK herd which is around 150,000 animals.

Alpacas are hardy, generally quiet animals with a life span of fifteen to twenty years and an adult weighs between fifty and eighty five kilograms and is about five feet tall to the top of the head.

They are herd animals and should not be kept on their own. Females are ready for mating when they are fourteen to eighteen months old, and the gestation period is just over eleven months. The young are called cria.

Alpacas are relatively easy to keep and graze well in the UK provided all poisonous trees and plants are removed from the field. Clean water and readily available hay is essential in the winter and a supplementary coarse mix feed will need to be fed to heavily pregnant females and young stock.

They do not require special fencing but barbed wire should not be used and a field shelter must be provided. Alpacas need their feet and teeth trimmed regularly, and are usually vaccinated against clostridial diseases and wormed when necessary.

The twenty two fleece colours range from black, grey, brown and fawn in different

Inquisitive Alpacas

Worm Farming

The worm most commonly used in commercial farming in the UK is Dendrobaena Veneta or the earth worm. It digests organic waste, produces good compost and can also be used as fish bait.

Worms are self propagating and digest copious amounts of waste; however they do need feeding green or other wastes, watering, and protection from predators.

Worms can be propagated in plastic stacking boxes, or in larger systems of semi-permanent rectangular timber box beds, which are

Domestic wormery

Worms in their element

normally covered in plastic so that the worm is encouraged to work in the top layer. In the UK breeding and composting are normally done in 'worm beds' that are outdoors.

The worms can be sold as bait for anglers or dehydrated for use in fish and poultry feed. Marketing and packaging can be time consuming and expensive.

The worms are sold to the composting industries and this is known as vermiculture. Many local authorities are now using worms for the recycling of domestic waste to produce compost and this is known as vermicomposting.

Worm farmers may dispose of biodegradable waste for other businesses and then sell the compost (worm castings).

They can also make an income from selling vermicomposting starter kits to individual householders.

Trout Farming

Rainbow Trout, which are native to North West America, dominate fresh water aquaculture. A Danish entrepreneur introduced fish farming to the UK in the 1950s and there are now about three hundred and sixty trout farms. Brown, Golden and Blue Trout are other farmed varieties, although in smaller quantities.

Most are produced for the table and farmed in fresh water tanks, ponds, raceways and netting cages. Netting cages are prominent in Scottish lochs. Sea cages are used for a small quantity of fish. Some fish are produced for re-stocking fisheries.

Fish farms may handle one stage of the fish cycle or larger farms may complete the whole process including gutting, filleting, smoking and packing. Hatcheries keep brood stock and the ova (eggs) hatch into fry which are sold on to fingerling (small fish) producers

Trout ponds

who rear them until they are large enough to be grown on by table producers or re-stockers.

A good water flow with a sufficient oxygen level is essential to ensure the health of the fish. Trout are harvested when they reach seven to eight months of age and weigh three hundred to four hundred grams.

Some farms offer ponds where visitors can fish for a fee, which is known as 'Put and Take'.

Although at first glance this appears to be an easy way for farmers to diversify into another business, maintenance and labour costs can be high as it is an all-year-round activity.

Game

Shooting plays an important economic role in rural areas where it supports not only landowners and gamekeepers but others in trades that supply the industry.

Gamebirds reared on specialist game farms in the UK are released into the countryside each year to re-stock shoots where people pay to shoot the birds. This practice has been carried out for a long time and can also result in better management and replanting of

woodland areas as cover for the birds. This in turn leads to more conservation habitats for other species.

Pheasant and partridge are the birds most commonly reared although some farms may raise wild mallard duck. Many farms will have a breeding flock that are penned for the breeding season, which starts in February.

Some hatching eggs may be imported from Europe but they are generally hatched in separate incubators to prevent cross contamination in the case of disease. Pheasant and partridge take twenty four days to hatch, mallard twenty eight days.

Chicks and ducklings start to feed within a day of hatching and are fed on cereal crumbs;

Pheasant rearing pen

they progress on to grower pellets. The rations are formulated by game feed companies to suit each species.

Most chicks are reared under electric hen brooders and as soon as possible they are given access to grass runs to harden off. By four to five weeks of age they will no longer require artificial heat.

The birds are sold on to shoots as day old chicks or as poults (young feathered birds), pheasants when they are seven weeks old and partridge at twelve weeks.

In large shoots, gamekeepers take over the care of the bought-in or estate-hatched birds. Until they are acclimatised, they are confined and fed in predator proof pens or runs in the area where they are to be released, The gamekeeper will continue to put feed out when they have been released into the countryside to encourage them to stay in the area.

Ducklings are reared with an artificial brooder inside a wire run. At around seven weeks, wheat or barley may be introduced into their diet. Only a small number of ducks are reared, compared with pheasants.

Only a proportion of the game reared is actually shot, the rest will continue to live in the wild and go on to reproduce naturally in subsequent years.

Grouse shooting is also a significant business, especially in Scotland on managed moors. Other gamebirds and waterfowl are ptarmigan (Scotland only) common snipe, woodcock and geese.

Deer and wild boar are also shot on farms and estates as part of organised shoots.

Wild rabbits used to be a welcome addition to the British diet but many are shot as vermin now and left where they fall. Some are caught with ferrets and may reach a local butcher or restaurant. Most of the rabbit we eat in the UK is imported and we no longer farm rabbits on any large scale.

Cock and hen pheasants in breeding pens

The Abattoir: How animals are killed

Virtually all farm animals that are destined for the food chain will be slaughtered and processed in an abattoir or slaughterhouse.

Some abattoirs handle one species of animal or bird, for example just chickens or deer. This is because different handling equipment is used for different animals. It also avoids cross contamination.

Animals may be transported straight from the farm to a local abattoir by the farmer or by a livestock haulier. Sometimes they can be bought at a fatstock market and transported directly to the abattoir.

Large commercial producers and some smaller specialist producers will have an abattoir on site. Supermarkets also own their own abattoirs and have contracts with farmers to provide a regular supply of animals for killing. Animals must be fit and clean (free from faeces) before they go for slaughter.

Dressing out meat

The way in which animals are caught, handled and transported to their slaughter is an important factor in ensuring the best meat possible. But, more importantly, safe and humane handling guarantees the welfare of the animals themselves.

Journey times should be as short as possible. Stressed animals do not perform well and they should always be treated humanely. The same applies when animals are unloaded at the abattoir. Every abattoir in the UK operates under the supervision of an Official Veterinary Surgeon whose job is to inspect the animals as they arrive.

Once the animals are unloaded in to holding pens they are guided to a stunning area. There are three types of stunning method, electrical, carbon dioxide, and captive bolt stunning.

In the case of sheep they are physically carried to a stun cradle and held in place by the slaughterman, while a second slaughterman discharges an electric stun to the animal's head to render it unconscious.

The slaughterman then 'sticks' the animal. This is the term used for cutting the jugular arteries to remove the blood, at which point the animal is dead. Whilst on the stun cradle the fleece is loosened from the legs and breast. The animal is then hung on a metal hook and the entire fleece (with skin) is removed.

The fleeces are stored, and will be collected for tanning. The carcass is washed and then split open and eviscerated. This means the intestines and stomach are removed. They are placed in a bin for safe disposal at a later time.

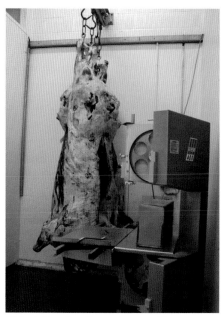

Sides of beef and a cutting machine

The offal, heart, liver and lungs are left attached to the throttle (throat) for inspection of the whole carcass by a Meat Hygiene Inspector. If approved, the carcass is stamped with the abattoir's unique number to ensure traceability of the meat and show that it is fit for human consumption. The carcass is then hung to cool in a refrigerated room.

It may be butchered (cut) into joints, chops etc at the abattoir, or transported to retail outlets, as whole or half carcasses, in refrigerated vehicles. The process is similar for most animals.

Cattle are not lifted manually. They are stunned with a captive bolt stun gun and the head and spinal cord are removed from all cattle. They are discarded after they have been inspected for signs of disease by the Meat Hygiene Inspector. After a further inspection of the dressed carcass it will be stamped as fit for human consumption.

Pigs are directed to the stunning area through a solid sided race which should be wide enough for two pigs to walk together. Most of the pig is used as only the blood and internal organs are removed.

Birds are transported in crates and on arrival at the abattoir or processing plant are inspected by an Official Veterinary Surgeon. They are hung upside down by their legs in shackles on a moving chain which progresses either to an electric bath, into which they are dipped to stun them, or gas is used to stun the birds. This is done to make them insensible to pain and stress.

The moving chain carries on to an automatic neck cutter and the birds are bled. Then they are dipped in a tank of scalding water to help loosen the feathers which makes plucking easier. They are mechanically plucked, and eviscerated, the carcass is washed and cooled then rested to ensure tenderness.

They may be packed and used as whole birds or divided into portions depending on the retail market.

High fencing for handling deer to the abattoir

The Lie of The Land

How History Created Britain's Farming Landscape

Despite being the product of millions of years of geological activity, alteration and erosion it is only during the last ten thousand years that the Britain of today becomes recognisable.

The glaciers of the last Ice Age retreated, exposing the land which was at first a barren waste until plants began to colonise. The melting glaciers fed into the oceans, flooding the valleys around Britain and separating it from Ireland and continental Europe.

With the warming climate, vegetation quickly established itself across Britain, with scrubby hazel and grasslands replaced in succession by oak and other broadleaf woodland. This was not a primaeval wildwood blanketing the whole of Britain, as it would not have covered the higher hilltops and may not have been well-established on the lighter soils of the chalk lands.

At this time, between ten thousand and six thousand years ago, people survived by gathering wild foods, hunting and fishing. Then the first farmers started clearing the woodland and agriculture was under way.

At Star Carr in the Vale of Pickering in Yorkshire, a waterlogged site has been found next to a former lake which provides

Antler headdress from Starr Carr in Yorkshire found with first evidence of farming in Britain

evidence of the seasonal exploitation of waterfowl, the taking of Red Deer and also the earliest evidence in Britain for the use of domestic animals, in this case the remains of a dog.

People do not appear to have lived in permanent settlements but moved around the landscape exploiting seasonally available plants and animals. This nomadic lifestyle begins to change around six thousand years ago when new plants and animals were introduced from the continent. For the first time we can see evidence of the cultivation of emmer wheat and barley, pulses such as beans and the breeding of sheep and goats.

Locally, cattle and pigs were also domesticated, and evidence points to the

Men-an-Tol in Cornwall, a megalith thought to be part of a tomb or barrow

establishment of more permanent territories, but farming appears to have supplemented the fisher-gatherer-hunter economy. The people of this period, between 6,000 and 4,500 years ago, made

Celtic Fields, Burderop, Wiltshire - an example of an early field system

Dartmoor reave at Saddlesborough

started to settle in hamlets of roundhouses with the formal laying out of fields and drove ways. Some modern field systems, such as the area around Scole and Dickleburgh in the Waveney Valley of southern Norfolk, are based on these ancient boundaries.

The best examples of these earliest fields are the Dartmoor reaves, a collection of denuded field walls with associated settlement remains. The largest spread of these fields is nine kilometres from end to end, and forms part of one of the best preserved prehistoric landscapes in Western Europe.

The survival of the prehistoric landscapes of Dartmoor is attributed to the arrival of wetter and windier conditions some 2,800 years ago. This forced people to make clearings in the lowlands in order to settle there and these can still be observed in the chalk lands of Wessex where the earthen banks of fields, denuded by later ploughing, are known as 'Celtic fields'.

Over 400 years the Roman occupation of southern Britain led to radical changes in the rural economy. The Roman authorities introduced a monetary system and a market-based economy. Former tribal lands were taken over, often forcibly, by private owners on villa estates (basically farms). New Roman roads facilitated easy access from the estates for crops and animals to be transported to market.

a lasting mark on the landscape. They constructed megalithic tombs, earthen barrows, hilltop enclosures and henge monuments, including Stonehenge.

Modern roads and field boundaries in some cases respect these monuments by going around them, but in other places the stones collected together at these sites became a handy quarry for road and wall building. Between 4,500 and 2,800 years ago, domesticated crops and animals became the dominant source of food. People

The Romans introduced a coulter and a heavy iron bar-share on the plough which meant that even more of the landscape could be turned over to crop production. Also, for the first time, farmers had access to iron-tipped spades, rakes and scythes.

Norfolk Dykes helped drain the Fens for grain production

The writings of the Classical authors show that Britain was considered a bread basket and was a good source of slaves and hunting dogs. During the Roman period the now familiar divide between city dwellers and country folk developed, although Scotland, Wales and southwest England below Exeter were relatively untouched.

In these places subsistence farming supplemented by some trading remained the norm. With more specialist trades emerging, and a greater proportion of people conducting them in towns, a need for the supply of food to the towns developed.

The Roman period also saw major reclamation of the East Anglian fens, with drainage on a large scale through the construction of dykes. Grain production appears to be the most significant reason for this reclamation.

When the Romans abandoned Britain it led to the desertion of towns and villas and a return to tribal or petty kingdom politics, a period of subsistence economics and uncertainty.

From the continent Angles, Saxons and Jutes settled in Eastern Britain, and raiding Vikings settled in Northern England. Wales was ruled by Welsh Princes and in the south of England Saxon kingdoms united under King Alfred the Great (871-899AD). Gradually urban centres became settled again, many in the ruins of former Roman towns. Estates and farms were resurrected and made use of the Roman roads.

Shortly after the Norman Conquest, the Domesday Book (1086) recorded the amount of land held by individuals and the taxable rates applicable to that land. We can see from Domesday that England was already organised in counties, most of which we would recognise today. Counties were further divided into fiefs and within fiefs were hundreds.

Within the hundreds were the farmed estates. This is a system which had become set in place during the Saxon period. Domesday also recorded the size and types of land held, using the measure of the hide (sixty to one hundred and twenty acres), and the number of ploughs and oxen owned.

The Domesday survey tells us that approximately thirty five per cent of the area of England was arable land, thirty per cent was pasture, fifteen per cent woodland and wood pasture and one per cent meadows. The other nineteen per cent was accounted for by uplands, fens, houses, gardens and wasteland.

Resources from each land type were all necessary for the functioning of the estate or farm and each were managed in specific ways to maintain them. It is therefore useful to consider each type in turn.

Arable and Pasture

There is a long history in Britain of dividing the land by hedges and walls to make fields: the boundaries could protect crops from animals or they could keep

The Vile Rhossili, an open field system on the Gower Peninsula, showing strips and furlongs once owned by different farmers

Corn Ditches, walls with a ditch, stopped animals reaching crops

Due to the ploughing of strips of land instead of a whole area, ridge-and-furrow wave-like undulations became etched on the landscape. The distinctive ridge-and-furrow was formed by the use of an asymmetric mouldboard drawn by the oxen in the narrow strips. Despite the later enclosure of the open fields evidence of their existence remains abundant in the landscape, and is best observed in low winter sunlight when shadows reveal the corrugated ground surface.

animals enclosed. They also provided convenient parcels to rent or own.

In the Middle Ages the parcels of land were replaced in much of Britain by much larger 'open fields' characterised by strip cultivation. A few examples survive, such as the Rhossili open fields on the tip of the Gower Peninsula in South Wales or that at Braunton in North Devon, Laxton in Nottinghamshire and Soham in Cambridgeshire.

Open fields were divided into long strips: the field itself belonged to a village or township and strips were divided among the farmers. Blocks of strips were named furlongs and all farmers within each furlong planted the same crop. They also left adjacent strips fallow – ploughed but not planted - at the same time every second, third or fourth year. At any one time a quarter of the arable land of England was fallow.

After cropping or in fallow years stock were allowed to graze the stubble and weeds which preserved pasture by leaving the root structures intact. Their dung also improved the fertility of the soil.

In some rare examples the strips themselves, presumably where they were sold off as individual parcels, have been fossilised in field boundaries, leaving small groups of long thin fields which stand out in the modern landscape.

In the middle of the fourteenth century one-third of England was covered by open fields. By the early eighteenth century half of these had been sold and enclosed. The majority of the surviving open fields were removed by the late nineteenth century through a series of Enclosure Acts.

The resulting fields are a distinctive, perhaps now typical, feature of the lowland British landscape. Enclosure Commissioners imposed a grid pattern of large (at least by earlier standards) straight-edged fields, often apparently oblivious to local topography. Between 1750 and 1850 some two hundred thousand miles of hedges were planted.

The earlier field boundaries may often be observed on maps or aerial photographs as clusters of curved lines forming unorganised field boundaries with evidence of a farm or village at the centre. Many of these villages became deserted over time due to a variety of factors: the Black Death of the mid fourteenth century, the rearing of sheep for industrial-scale wool production, and migration from the countryside to the developing industrial towns and cities.

The best documented deserted village is that of Wharram Percy in the Yorkshire Wolds, where archaeological excavations have revealed the complete village - the gardens or tofts of the individual houses, the 'infields' for cultivation and the 'outfields' for stock animals, two manor house complexes and the still standing ruins of a church.

Infields and outfields were often divided by a boundary known as a 'cornditch,' which was a wall or hedge with a ditch on its outer side to further deter animals from gaining access to the crops.

The Answer's in the Name

Many of the fields of today retain the names they were given one thousand or so years ago. With knowledge of the field names, which can be found on old maps and deeds, it is possible to build a vivid picture of past landscapes. When agriculture was so central to rural life, local people used a wide range of descriptive names which also acted as a guide to finding your way around the locality.

The Church owned much land and many field names reflect this, such as Glebe, Church Meadow and Parsons Wick. An 's' on the end of a field name such as Fosters End or Baileys Bottom tells us the family that once owned it.

The action of ploughing on slopes created terraces known as lynchets. Gravity moved the ploughed soil down the slope and piled it against the lower boundary. Strip fields are often preserved as lynchets, including the reversed 's' shape formed by the need to turn the oxen team in a wide curve. Strip lynchets are a particular feature of the chalk lands of southern Britain. In wetter areas and in smaller fields, ridge-and-furrow type features may have been formed by the shovelling of earth in linear piles to provide drainage for the soil and are known as 'daisy beds'.

Some Common Field Names

Lower Beer	Woodland producing acorns and beech nuts to feed pigs
Rack Park	Where wool was hung out to dry
Rials Field	Means Royal person
Meads	Fields near streams
Quillett	Small hamlet or village
Cleave or Cleeve	Steep slope
Silver Field	Site of old mine
Sweet Field	Fertile land
Hunger Down	Poor land

The gorse on this field at Painsford Farm shows why it was called Lower Furze Park

The map shows the field names at Painsford Farm in South Devon, where one of the authors of this book lives today. On a Particulars of Sale document for this farm dated about 1799, Rick Park was called Rack Park, Higher Marl Park was Marble Park and Mumps Park was Monks Park

1. Old Orchard
2. Wood Waste
3. Kitchen Orchard
4. Garden
5. Garden Orchard
6. Fountain Orchard
7. Ham Orchard
8. South Water Wood
9. Wood
10. Wilderness
11. Mill Field
12. Wood
13. Coppice
14. Two Acres
15. Higher Meadow
16. Plantation
17. Plantation
18. Lower Marl Park

Daisy Beds at Struan Portree on the Isle of Skye

Beyond the areas of open-field cultivation stood arable and pastoral lands enclosed with walls or hedges, the choice of which was determined by the availability of resources. In the Peak District of Derbyshire, stone walls survived as the dominant boundary type, some dating from Roman times.

Some stone walls evolved into hedges as plants and trees colonised them. It is generally accepted that hedges can be dated using English botanist Max Hooper's rule that the number of tree species in a thirty yard section of hedgerow correlates with centuries in age.   A hedge with eight species, for example, can be estimated at 800 years old.

But the Shapwick Landscape Project in Somerset found that a better indicator of antiquity came from identifying the diversity of insects and invertebrates resident in a hedgerow.

Woodland

The importance of woodland is sometimes overlooked in the study of early agriculture. But we know that woodland was actively 'farmed' in order to provide raw materials, fuel and fodder.

The historical importance of woodland can often be identified through the current presence of an earthen bank with a steep external side facing into a ditch as a defence, with the internal side of the bank being more gently sloped as an easy exit for any animals which had found access. Such a bank and ditch may in the present day be an archaeological feature in the landscape where the woods have completely disappeared, or it may surround shrunken

Coppiced Hazel

Pollarded Willow

Bonawe Furnace in Scotland burned oak and ash

animals, and much is now made of their importance in our industrial heritage.

Heritage, in all its guises, is big business, and the National Trust and its sister organisations are major landowners who often attempt to re-instate something closer to a pre-industrial type of farming. Such attempts are further supported by the government, which recognises the importance of the countryside for tourism and leisure.

Ken's view

The photograph below shows a small segment of the Harbourne Valley in the South Hams of Devon. The farming is agro-pastoral and the large square fields with planted hedgerows are the consequence of the Enclosure Acts post-1750. The far hillside shows that a lane, now a green lane, was preserved at this time. Later desire for larger fields is evident on the nearest hillside where the grubbing out of hedge has left the peculiar zig-zag formation. The tree-filled depression on the opposite valley side appears to be the location of a small, now disused, quarry. In the valley bottom the field boundaries form a funnel shape which may betray the former existence of a drift-way for bringing stock in from unenclosed land in to the valley bottom.

Ken's View: a typical farming landscape in South Devon

The Way We Farm

A typical mixed farm with barns, milking parlour and farmhouse cheek by jowl

Britain has a temperate climate, good soils, plenty of rain and a record of efficient and profitable farming. Yet we produce only half of the food we eat, most British people live in towns and cities divorced from the countryside and less than one percent of the population work in agriculture.

This is hardly surprising when even a large arable or dairy farm can be run by two or three people using computer-controlled combine harvesters or robotic milking parlours. But it is also reflects the changes in agriculture over the last fifty years, and the economic pressure on UK farmers posed by cheaper imported food.

Hundreds of dairy farmers, for instance, have stopped farming because the price they get for their milk is less than it costs to produce it. Similar trends can be seen in other products, from cauliflowers to hops to cherries.

And the traditional mixed farm, in which cereals, vegetables, legumes and livestock are rotated in order to protect and enrich the soil, has been replaced by the specialist producer of grain, meat, milk or vegetables operating on a larger and more intensive scale.

The new generation of farmers, especially cereal and crop growers, are dependent on fertilisers and minerals to produce a good crop because animal manure or natural nitrogen from legumes such as beans or clover, is no longer available as part of the farm cycle.

In this chapter we look at the way different farmers have responded to the challenge of this new marketplace for food. From the

In schools we are told about the Agricultural Revolution of the 18th and 19th centuries which enclosed the land, mechanised planting and harvesting, improved crop rotation and improved the breeding of sheep, pigs and cattle. In so doing it enabled the country to be largely self-sufficient in feeding a population that trebled in a hundred years.

In some respects the country is now undergoing another agricultural revolution. This time the agents of change are the polytunnel, the climate-controlled glasshouse and the power of the supermarkets to control food price and quality.

traditional Cheshire dairy farmer selling his milk to a co-operative, the Yorkshire potato grower whose crop is largely used to make crisps to the giant tomato grower who lets his supermarket customer decide how many tomatoes he wants on each vine.

Thanet Earth in Kent, Britain's largest greenhouse complex, grows tomatoes, peppers and cucumbers

Apple Grower

At a time when orchards have been grubbed out all over the country, the apple orchards in the Wye valley at harvest time in September are a welcome blaze of green, yellow, red and russet.

There are 15 acres of dessert apples on Hill Farm, mainly Cox and Egremont Russetts, and 90 acres of cider apples with names like Michelin Seedling, Dabinett, and Harry Masters. One much sought-after variety, Kingston Black, is deep red and often used to make premium cider and cider brandy.

Britain largest cider company is based in neighbouring Hereford and Hill Farm is one of their contract suppliers.

> *"All things being equal you make more money growing dessert apples than cider apples, although the costs and risks are much higher,"* says Richard Wheeler, who has worked at Hill Farm for many years. *"But cider is your bread and butter, your banker if you like.*
>
> *"Quality is not such a big issue because they are all going for processing. Trees are bigger and therefore the fruit is less vulnerable to frost. With dessert apples you can have thirty seconds of hail and it will wipe out the crop."*

Richard says apple trees in England are flowering earlier than they used to – the third week of April rather than early May – but a strong healthy blossom does not guarantee a good crop of apples because damage may be caused by bad weather later.

Herefordshire

Size:	106 acres
Soil:	Sandy loam
Rainfall:	26 inches a year

Richard Wheeler with Egremont Russetts

Apples like Coxes, which store well, can be picked before they are ready to eat because they will mature slowly in storage. Others are picked fully ripe for immediate sale. Bramley cooking apples can be kept in storage for as long as a year.

Dessert apples are picked by hand, but cider apples are harvested by machines which shake the tree, "blow" the apples into rows, gather them from the ground and put them in trailers.

At Hill Farm, like most orchards, the apple trees tend to have a 20 year life cycle and produce the best crop in their middle years.

Arable farmer

Manor Farm is in many ways a typical family-run arable farm with large fields to accommodate the increased size of agricultural machinery, which in turn means fewer farmworkers are needed.

Algy Garrod grows 350 acres of wheat, 160 acres of spring barley and 50 acres of winter barley. Additionally, 240 acres of sugar-beet are grown for British Sugar with 160 acres of oil seed rape sold for oil production.

Algy grows 130 acres of 'grain' maize rather than forage types planted under a biodegradable cover and sown earlier to give it a chance to ripen.

To preserve the grain grown on arable farms in good condition the moisture content has to be controlled with driers that blow hot air through the corn. It is then stored in giant silos or purpose-built barns which protect it from vermin.

When Algy wanted to add value to his crops, his first venture was growing

Silos for storing grain, an essential feature of any large arable farm

Norfolk

Size:	1,000 acres
Soil:	Sand to chalk boulder clay
Rainfall:	28 inches a year

sunflowers to go with the grain maize to produce bird seed. Other alternative crops include red and white millet and Canary seed which comes from a grass.

Sunflowers are an important source of bird seed

This was the beginning of Bintree Bird Seed, which supplies a commercial seed market and a mixed corn ration for poultry.

Looking for a fresh challenge, Algy also put five special varieties of maize on trial to find one that would work in Norfolk for making popcorn. He found it, and the hand-picked maize, which is smaller than other varieties, is turned into natural popcorn and sold from the farm.

Algy says "I think the outlook is quite positive, food production is something we can't ignore. The biggest pain is the amount of red tape, the bain of my life. We are fortunate that we are supported and must not lose sight of that."

Asparagus Grower

Before they were drained, the Fens were more sea than land and the sandy silts left behind provide some of the most fertile farmland in England. Every crop seems to flourish. Nick and Ros Loweth grow wheat, sugar beet, rape, potatoes, pumpkins and courgettes on their completely flat fields near Boston.

But for eight weeks of the year they also cut asparagus for sale to restaurants, hotels and prestigious shops such as Fortnum and Mason. The crop is only grown on 20 acres of the farm, but the 40 tons they harvest each year sells at over £5 a kilo, which makes the brief English asparagus season (May and June) a very profitable one.

Lincolnshire

Size:	300 acres
Soil:	Sandy silt
Rainfall:	24 inches a year

The asparagus spears are cut by a sharp knive just below the soil and it can be back-breaking work for Nick and his four farmworkers. When the crop is plentiful a rig is used to move through the fields collecting the spears before they are graded and packed on the farm.

Nick says the most profitable way of selling asparagus is direct to the public by mail order or through their own farm shop.

Nic Loweth using a specialised rig to cut asparagus

Dairy Farmer

David Johnson and his silage clamp

<table>
<tr><td colspan="2">Cheshire</td></tr>
<tr><td>Size:</td><td>200 acres</td></tr>
<tr><td>Soil:</td><td>heavy clay</td></tr>
<tr><td>Rainfall:</td><td>24 inches a year</td></tr>
</table>

The best grazing for dairy cattle is in the west of the country where heavy rainfall encourages the grass to grow faster and more luxuriantly - the ideal conditions for the dairy cow, which is basically a machine for turning grass into milk.

Each of his 90 Holstein cows provides David Johnson with about 7,200 litres of milk a year on his 200 acre farm near Warrington. This is less than some intensively raised herds which will produce 10,000 litres a cow with additional feed but David prefers to farm in a traditional way, grazing the herd in summer, and giving them silage in the winter with additional forage such as kale or rape to supplement their diet.

"I calve one third of my cows in January and February, and the rest in July and August. Cows produce most milk at the beginning of their lactation so mine are producing most milk in the winter when supplies are less and I can take advantage of higher milk prices."

The cows have straw bedding and plenty of space when they come indoors in the winter. Milking is carried out in a traditional 8 abreast parlour with the stockman positioned between two rows of cows and able to keep a close eye on them.

But to cut down on labour and other milking costs David milks his herd once every 16 hours instead of twice a day. "It's the best decision I ever made," says David. "I've got a young family and I wanted to see them. We don't have to get up every morning and it's had no effect on our yield."

All his grass fields (or leys) are sown at five to nine year intervals – he has no permanent pasture – and he normally takes three grass cuts a year to make silage. In some fields David has planted a mixture of ryegrass, clover, peas and barley which he says make a specially nutritious silage. To save costs he stores all the silage in a "clamp" rather than baling it in plastic sheeting.

David only needs a small number of heifer calves to replace the adult cows that are lost each year. The rest of the calves are reared as beef cattle and sold at about 18 months.

Like other dairy farmers, David has to be careful about the amount of slurry and solid manure he spreads on his fields because he is in a Nitrate Vulnerable Zone where there is a danger of water contamination.

Hill Farmer

Situated in dramatic countryside near the Brecon Beacons, Pwll yr Hwyaid (Pool of the Ducks) is a family-run farm supporting three generations. The farm is in a Less Favoured Area (LFA) and is typical of Welsh hill farms where making a living is hard.

The Morgan family part-own and part-rent the land they farm.

> *"It is a way of life, we are always happy to go with the weather," says Huw Morgan. "You are your own boss and can take a day off in the worst conditions."*

The land rises to 1350 feet and has over a thousand ewes speckled on the hillsides, with a fifty strong beef suckler herd. The young cattle are sold at local markets to be fattened elsewhere.

The breeding ewes, known locally as Talybont on Usk Welsh ewes, are crossed with Cheviot rams, then crossed again with lowland rams to produce a better carcase. The sheep have their lambs in two batches in the spring. The lambs are sold to Waitrose and processed in the local abattoir at Llanidloes. The wool goes to the Wool Marketing Board.

The Morgans grow their own hay, silage and swede to feed their animals in the winter months. The land is fertilized with bought-in human manure which is spread in pellet form.

Pwll yr Hwyaid is part of the Tir Gofal (Land Care) agri-enviroment scheme for Wales.

Powys

Size:	400 acres
Soil:	Old red sandstone
Rainfall:	up to 118 inches a year

The Morgan family have over a thousand ewes

Tir Gofal was the first scheme in Europe which was aimed at promoting whole-farm conservation and management. There are four elements to the scheme: Habitat Conservation, Landscape Management, Historical and Archaeological Features and Access.

The farmer must sign a 10 year agreement to qualify for payments. Existing habitats and rights of ways must be preserved and boundaries, trees, historic sites and traditional buildings maintained.

The Morgan family have embraced the scheme wholeheartedly by laying hedges, repairing stone walls, double-fencing to provide an inner habitat, coppicing and planting traditional orchards.

Hop Grower

The Walker family have been growing hops for over a hundred years, but they are part of a declining industry. There are thought to be fewer than a hundred growers left in England.

The Walkers grow several different varieties including First Gold, Sovereign and Fuggles and they have increased the acreage devoted to dwarf hops which are easier to grow and harvest, are less vulnerable to high winds and need shorter poles and wires to support them.

Hops are now harvested by a machine which strips the flowers or cones from the vine and blows them into trailers. Back at the farm they are dried on trays to reduce the moisture content from 80% to about 12% and stored in 50 kilogram sacks known as zentners. Dried hops can be kept for up to a year before being used for brewing.

Worcestershire

Size:	57 acres
Soil:	Silty loam on clay
Rainfall:	27 inches a year

Traditional oast houses used to be used for drying but although they survive on the Walkers' farm, it is now more economic to dry the hops in large sheds equipped with kilns, gas burners, hoppers and conveyor belts.

"Unlike many crops, we find that when we have a high volume the quality of the hops is also better,"says John Walker.

"And during harvest in September some brewers - like the one at our neighbouring pub - like to make beer with green hops which have not been dried. They use the hops the same day they have been picked."

Hop field

Micro Leaf Grower

In his giant glasshouses in the Vale of Evesham Martin Boers propagates brassicas, aliums and strawberries from seed and cuttings for other growers, and grows salads and herbs as his family has done for many years.

But he has now taken his operation to a level that most farmers could never dream of. With the help of specialists from Holland, Germany and the UK, he has built a fully automated glasshouse and germination unit to produce "micro leaves."

Westland Nursery

These are very young salad leaves or herbs cut at the earliest possible stage when many of them have a higher nutrient content and a more intense flavour than mature leaves. Seeds are spread by machine on to moist sterile matting, then germinated in a special unit and moved around the glasshouse by computer to control the growing environment.

After ten to 30 days – the computer times the journey to fit the growing cycle of each variety – the matting tray returns to the "factory" for the tiny basil, chard, chive or

Basil and Micro Basil

" I was looking at our baby leaf salads and thought the market was ready for something different," says Martin Boers. "We played around with seeds, cell sizes and different varieties in our propagation unit and when I took some of the tiny leaves to Jamie Oliver's and a number of other London restaurants they just loved the intense flavour and the appearance of the leaves."

sorrel leaves to be cut by a fine saw and packed ready for distribution.

Westland Nurseries is the largest grower of micro leaves in the UK and they are sold mainly to the catering industry for salads and food garnishes. The high cost of the tiny leaves makes it uneconomic to turn them into sauces or other processed food.

Narcissi grower

Isles of Scilly

Size: 27 acres
Soil: Very sandy loam
Rainfall: 35 inches a year

Flowers bloom earlier in the Scillies than anywhere else in the UK. The Gulf Stream ensures frost-free winters in the tiny group of islands just 30 miles off the west coast of Cornwall and growers take advantage of this to produce early daffodils and narcissi.

Churchtown Farm on the island of St Martins specialises in farm-to-home postal delivery under the brand name Scent from the Islands. The first narcissi flower as early as September, and business reaches a peak at Christmas, when up to 20,000 boxes of flowers are picked, packed and posted to individual customers.

Grower Ben Julian says: "Scented narcissi are unique to the islands. They are not grown elsewhere in Britain because they cannot withstand the frost. Here they are bathed in the warm Gulf Stream and we have methods of warming the soil to encourage early flowering."

This includes covering a portion of the fields with polythene in May and June and lighting fires to blow smoke underneath it. From May to September Churchtown switches to the production of scented pinks, planted in grow bags to control weeds and ensure more effective irrigation on an island in which fresh water is in short supply.

The farm employs 20 full-time staff and 30 extra workers at peak periods. It sells 2.8 million flowers a year.

Picking narcissi on Churchtown Farm

Organic Farmer

Devon

Size: 850 acres
Soil: Clay loam over slate
Rainfall: 45 inches a year

Guy Watson with Riverford squash

Devon is the centre of a nationwide business that now incorporates neighbouring farm co-operatives as well as sister farms in Cambridgeshire, Yorkshire, Hampshire, Cheshire and Kent.

Pest-eating insects such as hoverfly, lacewings and ladybirds are encouraged to breed, which keeps down destructive insects such as aphids. Riverford has its own organic herd of dairy cows – an important source of manure for the vegetable fields.

On organic farms no synthetic fertilisers or pesticides are used and the emphasis is on working with nature rather than dominating and replacing it.

Green manures, legumes and mulches return nutrients to the soil and the organic farmer encourages predators that eat pests.

About 5% of the farmed land in the UK is considered organic, but most farmers use organic methods when they can - no farmer wishes to spend money on fertilizers or food supplements if he can avoid it.

The Watson family have been at the forefront of organic farming in Britain for over 20 years. Their 850 acre Riverford Farm in the beautiful Dart Valley in

Vegetable Box Scheme

Guy Watson is one of the pioneers of the scheme whereby boxes of fresh vegetables are delivered to thousands of homes throughout the country every day. But he is realistic about what can be achieved in the British climate.

"We encourage customers to make the most of local and seasonal produce without being so dogmatic that we drive them back to the supermarkets. The small percentage that we import includes all the citrus and tropical fruit that won't grow in this country."

Riverford Organic Vegetables deliver boxes of fresh vegetables to 45,000 homes across the UK each week. To avoid "food miles" the boxes are distributed from six regional centres, each supplied by local organic farms trading under the Riverford banner.

Ninety per cent of the vegetables in Riverford Veg Boxes are home grown. This is near 100% in late summer and drops to 60% in late spring.

Without combine harvesters, bringing in the cereal harvest would be too labour intensive

And many farmers would be the first to admit that the appearance, if not the quality, of modern farm buildings is nothing to be proud of.

But despite the change in the character and use of farm buildings, they are still normally found in close proximity to the house in which the farmer and his family live. A cluster of barns, silos, shelters for machinery, a milking parlour and grain stores make up the farmstead, the heart of any farm.

Mechanisation has changed not only farming itself, but the visual appearance of farmland. The traditional threshing barn has been replaced, not by another building but by a machine. The combine harvester cuts, threshes and winnows the grain and leaves the straw to be collected and baled by another machine. Job done.

Successful farming in the 21st century owes much more to the effective use of an increasingly complex range of agricultural machinery than it does to traditional farm buildings. These have been replaced by multi-purpose sheds, often prefabricated and made of very "untraditional" materials: concrete, corrugated steel, painted aluminium and plastic.

Add to this the grain silo, the black plastic silage bale, the giant glasshouse and the polytunnel and we have to recognise that the modern face of farming is not always a thing of beauty.

In this section we describe the most common agricultural buildings and machines, but we also look at some traditional farm buildings that do remain, even if most of them are now derelict or used for other purposes.

Barns

The word "barn" comes from the old English for a barley store, and it is a roofed building for storing grain, straw or hay. Traditional barns are some of the most beautiful buildings in the countryside, but modern ones are much more functional and normally made of metal, concrete or plastic.

Dutch barns

Hay Barns

Hay needs to be kept dry and traditional haystacks were not a reliable means of storing large quantities of hay once crop rotation greatly increased the haymaking potential of traditional farms. The solution was open barns to provide adequate ventilation but with roofs to keep out the rain.

Those with a fixed roof, often with iron supports, and no side walls were known as Dutch Barns.

Some hay barns had solid brick walls at either end with patterned ventilation slits and others had roofs where the height could be adjusted to suit the amount of hay being stored. Hay barns can be found throughout the UK, although they may now be used to store other agricultural produce and implements, not just hay.

Threshing Barns

Before the arrival of threshing machines and combine harvesters, the job of threshing grain from sheaves of wheat or barley was backbreaking and monotonous work carried out by labourers throughout the winter using hand flails. Barns had to be high enough to allow men to swing the flail, and the threshing floor hard enough to withstand the constant beating.

Threshing barn

Tithe barn

produce went to monasteries rather than individual priests, and some of the largest tithe barns were associated with monasteries and colleges. Tithes in kind were abolished in 1836.

Barn Conversions

Very few barns are still in use for their original purpose. Thousands have been demolished or left to fall into disrepair, but most have been converted into private homes and offices. The best conversions manage to retain the character of the original buildings.

The grain then had to be winnowed or tossed in the air to remove the chaff. Tall doors made sure there was enough light for the beaters to see all the grain on the floor. Low wooden boards – or thresholds – were placed in the doors to stop grain escaping.

Tithe Barns

For hundreds of years the church was able to levy a tithe on all farmland to pay for the upkeep of the parish priest or rector. A tithe was one tenth of agricultural produce, and the tithes of grain and hay were stored in large barns built for the purpose. Often the

Bank Barns

This is the name given to barns built on a slope or bank in mixed farms in hillier parts of the country. The top floor was normally a threshing barn and a grain store reached from the field or road, and the lower floor, entered from the farmyard, housed cattle, horses and carts. Hay or straw could be dropped through hatches into the cowshed below.

Bank barn in winter

Cattle Sheds

From outside, modern farm buildings can look very similar and it may not be clear what their function is. They are usually large, and whether they are built of brick, concrete, wood, plastic or metal they can resemble an industrial unit dropped into the countryside.

Modern cow shed from outside

But a row of slowly moving cows, or the muddy mess they leave behind, makes it easy to spot a cowshed, especially one used by dairy cows, who come in and out twice a day to be milked.

Cattle are usually housed in open sheds in which they are free to move around. There will be rows of stalls or cubicles in which they can choose to lie or stand on a bed of straw or an inert material such as silver sand.

There needs to be plenty of ventilation but the biggest consideration in the design of a cattle shed is how to dispose of their waste. One dairy cow produces about 50 litres of urine a day, and 30 litres of dung. This excrement has to be removed each day.

Most cowsheds will have a solid floor and a channel into which liquid can run to a slurry tank outside the shed. The floor will be cleaned once or twice a day by an automatic yard scraper or a scraper pushed by a tractor. Over the winter a cow housed inside will need about a ton of straw for bedding, and this too has to be periodically cleaned away.

Floors need to be non-slip, and there will be large troughs for water, hay and silage. A milking parlour will be separated from the cattle shed, even if it is under the same roof. (see page 89)

Cattle used to be kept in stalls and tethered loosely to a post which enabled them to stand, eat or lie down, head-on to a feeding passage running the length of the house. A loose feeding box in the passage and a hay rack above the stall provided food.

As in modern-day sheds, the floor of the cow house had to be on a gentle incline to enable waste to be scraped away and urine to drain into a channel. Animal dung would be removed and taken to a midden, where it was stored, often under cover.

In the earliest cow houses hay would be stored in a loft above, which meant the space for cattle was reduced, the roof was low and the house was poorly lit and ventilated. But once hay became a smaller part of the winter diet of cattle it was often stored in separate barns and cow houses became aerier and lighter.

The term shippen was sometimes used for a cow house, especially where dairy cows were kept to be milked.

Shippen

Field Shelters

Sheep and cattle are often left to graze in fields a long way from the farmstead. Small barns and shelters erected at convenient outposts of the farm enable hay, straw and other feedstuffs to be kept close to where they are needed. Some field buildings also enable livestock to take shelter or be separate from other animals.

Round Feeder

To make silage or hay available to cattle to eat, while ensuring each animal is able to access a similar amount, farmers will put circular metal feeding troughs in the field or the farmyard.

Gloucester cattle and round feeder

Glasshouses

The term "protected" is used to describe the vegetables, soft fruit, herbs and flowers in the UK which are grown under cover, normally in large greenhouses.

To the passer-by, a commercial glasshouse will appear very large and very high, and this is to provide adequate ventilation. Layers of heat build up under glass and this needs to be kept away from the growing plants.

Most of the vegetables grown in greenhouses are still planted in soil, growbags or plastic "modules" with several plants or pots. But the new generation of intensive growers are using rockwool or raising their products hydroponically, in a liquid enriched with nutrients. In highly specialised glasshouses, such as those growing micro-herbs (see page 163) the preferred growing material is matting.

And instead of planting their crops on the ground, an increasing number of growers plant them at table-top level, which makes handling them much easier.

Apart from sprinkler systems, other technologies widely used in glasshouses are sensors to monitor soil humidity, climate control programmes to raise and lower temperature and carbon dioxide supply, and combined heat and power plants to save energy costs.

Many commercial glasshouses are imported from Holland, some of them using second hand structures, and they are growing bigger every year.

Thanet Earth is 55 hectares of glass in Kent producing tomatoes, cucumbers and peppers. The seven glasshouses will eventually take up the equivalent of 80 football pitches. Artificial lighting will enable tomatoes to be cropped 52 weeks of the year.

Large glasshouse at Thanet Earth

Polytunnels

Polytunnels

Growing vegetables and fruit such as celery, cucumber, strawberries and tomatoes has been revolutionised by the development of polythene covers, generically known as polytunnels.

Easy to erect, they protect sensitive crops from bad weather and by providing a warmer environment they extend the growing season. They also make it possible to grow exotic crops such as chillies.

Polytunnels may be permanent, built with a strong enough structure to withstand most weather conditions. Temporary tunnels – the most common are known as Spanish tunnels

- are taken down in the winter and put up in the Spring once the likelihood of strong winds has passed. Spanish tunnels can be blown over by gales.

Polytunnels are normally erected with several interconnected bays, with the opportunity to open the "skirt" at the edges to improve ventilation. In telescopic versions the hoops can be dropped down the supporting legs and the polythene dug into the soil to give a better seal.

Crops raised in polytunnels can be planted into the soil, grown in bags or troughs or use a table top growing system.

Silage Clamps

In a country full of beautiful barns and longhouses the most important agricultural "building" for many farmers nowadays is a pile of rotting grass covered in black plastic sheeting and weighed down by car tyres or railway sleepers.

A thing of beauty it isn't, but for dairy farmers the silage clamp is the main "larder" for cows over the winter. Making good quality silage from grass, clover, maize and other green plants is one of their most important tasks.

The cut grass is dropped into a shallow pit, usually with solid walls on three sides, compressed to remove the air and covered in polythene sheeting. The process continues until the clamp is full, when it is covered completely with polythene and weighed or tied down with a net to stop the plastic flapping and air getting in.

Over the course of the winter the air in the clamp is used up, the grass ferments and the pile contracts under its own weight. The "pickled grass" is fed to cattle on its own or with some nutrients added.

Care must be taken to stop silage effluent escaping into rivers and streams. This is why a special tank is always built next to the clamp to trap escaping liquid.

Farmers also preserve silage in large cylindrical bales, and piles of stacked silage bales wrapped in black plastic are more visible to most passers-by than the silage clamp, which is usually out of sight at the back of the farmstead.

Maize silage clamp with buck rake

Some Traditional Farm Buildings

Dairy

Making butter and cheese needed a cool, well-ventilated and spacious building where there was plenty of room for the storage of milk churns, for separating cream from the milk and for the process of churning milk into butter.

Where large quantities of cheese were made there also needed to be room for the tuns or kettles in which milk was heated, the cheese press and racks for storing and turning the cheese.

A dairy could be a separate building in the farmstead, usually north facing with plenty of cold stone slabs to keep it cool, or part of the farmhouse.

Away from the dairy itself, the butterwell was a small stone structure, usually at a spring or bog, in which dairy products were kept cool on slate shelves.

Butterwell

And the ubiquitous churn stand was a platform of stone, brick or concrete built by the roadside for farmers to leave their milk churns for collection by dairies.

Dovecotes

Nowadays dovecotes are small, ornamental "houses on a pole" which can be bought

Traditional dovecote

from a garden centre or by mail order to keep half a dozen birds.

But in their heyday, dovecotes were homes to huge quantities of pigeons whose meat and eggs were an important part of the diet of landowners and their tenants. Pigeon manure was also highly valued.

Most had over 500 nesting boxes built into their round, octagonal, square or rectangular walls, providing accommodation for over a thousand birds.

Low doors at the bottom of the building discouraged the doves and pigeons from flying out, but allowed access to collect the eggs. This could be a complicated business, involving ladders and leaning posts, but round dovecotes without corners made collecting eggs much easier.

Engine Houses

To provide power to threshing barns, roundhouses (also known as gin gangs or wheel houses) were built next door where a horse would walk round and round "ganging" or pushing a shaft to turn a spindle which transmitted power to the threshing engine or "gin." Most engine houses were built in England where water power was less readily available than in other parts of the United Kingdom.

Granary

As farmers increased the amount of grain they produced they wanted to store it until it would fetch the best price. It had to be kept dry, well-ventilated and protected from rats and other vermin. The answer was a self-contained thatched or tiled building raised on a set of staddle stones to keep it clear of the ground.

Granary

The staddle stones were smooth pillars with a projecting cap, providing no grip for mice and rats. A removable platform, rather like a drawbridge, provided a gap between the steps and the granary door which was too wide for them to jump. Granaries were also built on top of cartsheds and stables.

Longhouse

Across much of Britain, animals and humans used to share the same dwelling, perhaps with the addition of a small barn.

Cattle would be tethered in one half of the house, with a drain in the end wall to allow waste to escape. The family accommodation was at the other end, sometimes with a cross-passage between the two halves of the building to allow the farmer to check on his livestock.

These longhouses were common in Devon and South Wales, where they are now much sought after as family homes.

Linhay

Very common in Devon and Cornwall, the linhay is a two-storey building open on one side. The ground floor provided shelter for cattle while the top floor was a hay loft. Piers of stone or wood at the front provided support to the top floor.

Linhay

Maltings

Converting barley into malt for brewing used to take place in malting kilns on the farm. The barley grain would be soaked in water for two days and then spread on the floor of the building to germinate. After a week or ten days the germinating barley would be dried in a kiln and stored for sale.

As the demand for malt grew, much larger premises were built away from the farm, often close to railway stations, or within breweries themselves. The furnaces heating the drying floor were fuelled by anthracite or charcoal.

Because malt used to be taxed, maltings were in effect "bonded" premises and windows were often barred to prevent the valuable product being stolen.

Oast House

Newly harvested hops must be artificially dried before they can be used for brewing (the exception being green hop beer). Traditionally this was carried out in hop kilns called oast houses which used charcoal furnaces to heat a drying floor on which the green hops were spread. The conical roof of the oast house covers a tapered flue and it is topped by a rotating cowl through which the fumes escape.

Oast houses were often constructed in pairs or, as in this example from Herefordshire, threes. We are not aware of any oast house in Britain which is still used to dry hops. Most are now unused or converted to private homes.

Oast houses

Pigsty

Pigs are hardy and productive animals and before farmland was enclosed they would forage in the woods and scavenge on food left behind by other animals.

Selective breeding has produced pigs which are more vulnerable to the cold, and low level loose boxes were developed to contain the animals and offer them more protection.

Pigsties were often built two or three abreast with a door leading on to a narrow yard, a slit for ventilation and a feeding trough. Pigs are strong animals and the walls of the yard had to be thick and tall.

In parts of Wales circular pigsties with conical roofs were built. Today pigs are kept in specially designed buildings and unlike barns or stables, traditional pigsties cannot easily be used for other purposes so few are retained.

Poundhouse

Hundreds of properties across the UK are still called "poundhouse" but it is unlikely that many of them fulfilled the true role of the poundhouse, which was to "pound" or pulverise apples to make cider.

These are mainly found in the south and south west of England. In moorland areas to the north of Britain stock pounds were used to retain livestock in areas of common grazing, in the same way that stray dogs are nowadays taken to "pounds," and the term poundhouse may have been used for houses next to stock pounds.

Stables

Horses were more valuable and fragile than other farm animals and their accommodation reflected this. Stables were tall and well ventilated, and each horse normally had a stall of its own with a manger (feeding trough) for oats and a metal or wooden rack to hold hay.

Most stables had a hay loft above with dormers or round holes in the walls ("pitching eyes") through which the hay could be "pitched" with a hay fork.

Norfolk stables converted into dwelling

Farm Machinery

The Tractor

It may be the favourite of every small boy, but the most widely used piece of agricultural equipment does not actually perform many farming jobs itself. The tractor provides power to the many machines that actually do the work. It pulls them, pushes them and, using "take-off" from the engine and hydraulics, enables them to operate. As the farm workhorse, it:

- Propels machines around the farm, usually by trailing them on a drawbar
- Provides rotary power through a power take-off shaft
- Lifts and moves equipment using hydraulic power

Almost all tractors are powered by four-stroke diesel engines, and most of them have four-wheel drive for greater grip. They are becoming bigger and heavier to cope with larger and more powerful equipment and on many occasions they will push and pull machinery at the same time.

The average engine size increases all the time. Over one hundred horse power is common, and the most powerful tractors have engines up to 500 hp. A wide range of gears is needed for different conditions and tasks, and very low gears – where the wheels turn no more than 20 rpm – are needed to pull heavy loads. Some automatic gearboxes may have 30 forward and reverse speeds.

To reduce the risk of slipping on wet ground, and ensure they don't overturn when pulling heavy equipment, farmers sometimes increase the ballast of tractors by adding iron weights to the front of the vehicle, or attach cast iron discs to the wheels. Another method of increasing traction, not often used in the new generation of large tractors with huge wheels, is to pump water into the tyres.

Power Take Off Shaft

Hydraulic pipes

Lifting arms

Draw bar

Farm equipment that is pulled by a tractor, such as a plough or a tipping trailer, usually needs to be raised or lowered several times a trip. This is a achieved by connecting the device to the tractor's hydraulic system. A pump sends oil to a ram or piston on the attached device, which lifts the load. When the device lowers under its own weight the oil is forced back into the tractor's oil reservoir.

Machinery is attached to the rear (or front) of the tractor using a three-point linkage and power take-off shafts. The device is pulled by the draw bar, but the load on the tractor is controlled by the top link and the lifting arms, which raise the device – a plough, for example - when it drops belows the required working depth. This reduces risk of the tractor toppling over.

One of the biggest problems with all farm machinery, but especially with tractors, is the pressure put on the soil by their great weight. This can lead to ground being compacted and reduced in quality.

To overcome this problem the pressure on the ground is reduced by using wider tyres, inflated to a minimum, and twin wheels. This is why tractor tyres, almost all with thick "chevron" treads, are so wide.

Soil compaction is best managed by using the lightest possible machines for the job, not using them when the ground is wet and avoiding too many tractor journeys over the same stretch of ground.

Link Boxes

Most common tractors have hydraulic rams to raise and lower a range of farm machinery. But one of the most common devices attached to the back of tractor is a small, metal carrying box, normally between four and six feet wide, which can be used for a variety of tasks around the farm. It may carry tools, small bales of hay or straw, or a cage for carrying livestock.

The Plough

The oldest form of cultivation is the use of a plough to prepare a field to sow a new crop. Once made of wood and pulled by oxen, the modern device is made of steel and when harnessed to a powerful tractor can plough 30 acres in a day.

Most ploughs used in Britain have two sets of "mouldboards", one which turns soils to the left and the other to the right. This enables the modern ploughman (the tractor driver) to plough continuously, reversing 180 degrees at the end of the field.

Ploughing "turns over" the top nine inches of soil and buries the weeds and stubble from the previous year's crop. It exposes the soil to the air and breaks up large clods.

Modern ploughs may have over ten mouldboards, each turning over a row of soil to create one furrow. A plough "share" cuts the ground horizontally, lifting the soil onto the mouldboard and there may be a coulter, or sharp blade, which cuts into the ground vertically ahead of the ploughshare.

Each mouldboard makes a furrow

Ploughing attracts scavenging birds

Cultivating the ground

The *harrow* is the traditional piece of equipment used to break up the soil after ploughing and turn it into a level seedbed. It uses spikes, called tines, or discs to create the tilth, the name given to fine, crumbly soil that is ready for sowing. The harrow can also be used to cover up the seeds once they are planted.

Very early harrows used bushes such as gorse or hawthorn for the same purpose. Now they are made of steel and pulled by tractors. Harrowing may have to be repeated, depending on the quality of the ploughing and the kind of seedbed required. Grass needs only a thin tilth, for instance, while maize can flourish in quite rough ground.

The traditional harrow is folded out to make a wide "rake" which is dragged behind a tractor. But many farmers are now using a power harrow which turns the soil as well.

More and more farmers are turning to *combination cultivators*, which use rows of rigid or spring-mounted tines to break up the soil less aggressively than ploughs, and discs and rollers to create a level seedbed.

Cultivators come in all shapes and sizes, and some of them are self-powered. They are favoured by farmers, especially those in cereal growing areas, who are using *minimum tillage* (see page 60) to "rip" the soil, rather than turning it with a plough.

Rotary Cultivators, sometimes known as *rotavators*, use 'L' shaped blades on a horizontal shaft powered by the tractor's power-take off to clean stubble, cut up weed and make a seedbed.

Sometimes seeds are drilled at the same time is the field is harrowed, especially when a

Chain harrow

Cultivator

A rotavator vibrates to help break up the ground

power harrow is being used. In March and April you will often see a tractor with a power harrow on the front and a seed drill at the rear.

Drills

The invention of the seed drill changed the face of agriculture as much as the combine harvester, although it took place much earlier. Scattering seed by hand onto an open field – or broadcasting – was a hit-and-miss affair. Most of the seed was wasted, hence the old proverb "one for the pigeon, one for the crow, one to wither and one to grow."

In 1700 a Berkshire farmer, Jethro Tull , was also the organist in his local church. It is thought that the organ pipes gave him the idea for a system of tubes for "aiming" seeds into regular spaced furrows in a field.

He designed a horse-drawn drill with a rotating cylinder. Grooves were cut into the cylinder to allow seed to pass from the hopper above to a funnel below. They were then directed into a furrow and a blade covered the seeds with soil. Because they were planted evenly spaced at the correct depth they germinated more successfully and the evenly spaced rows created by the drill made subsequent weeding much easier.

Seed drill

Seed in seed drill

Today's grain drills are much bigger, faster, and more expensive, and they are pulled by a tractor, not a horse. But they are only more elaborate versions of Jethro Tull's clever device. Some of them sow grain and fertilizer at the same time and some use a fan to blow the seeds into the soil rather than relying on gravity.

Seed drills vary according to the crop being sown. For crops that require more individual spacing, precision seeders are used. Instead of dropping seeds in a regular trickle, they use perforations in a wheel or belt to achieve more accurate distribution.

The three essential parts of a grain drill are a seed reservoir or hopper, a set of rollers which monitor and control the flow of seeds to the tubes and rows of blades or coulters which create holes to insert the seed.

Not all the tubes and coulters are used. Rows can be shut off so that when the crop grows, straight gaps or "tramlines" are left at regular interval across the field. This allows the farmer to use sprayers or fertilizer spreaders efficiently and without causing crop damage.

As approved by Jethro Tull !

Combine Harvester

If there were no combine harvesters there would be no wheat, barley or other grain produced in the UK.

The task of cutting the crop (reaping), separating the grain from the "ear" (threshing), removing dust or "chaff" (winnowing) and leaving stalks as straw requires too much labour to be cost effective.

The combine harvester does all four tasks, ejecting the grain into a trailer and leaving straw on the ground to be baled. And it does it so fast that cereals can be cut while the grain is at its best and before the weather turns. And if the summer has been wet, the combine can even collect cereals that have been flattened by rain and wind, so-called "laid crops."

Combines are also used to harvest seed crops like rape and linseed, and legumes like field beans and peas.

In a typical British summer, wet as it can be, there are normally only between 12 and 20 available working days during the harvesting period and getting the crop in quickly is a priority. This is why you will see, and hear, combine harvesters working through the

Some combines use GPS to ensure accurate harvesting

night if the farmer finds he has only a brief window of opportunity to get the grain in.

The most challenging job facing the combine operator is controlling the height at which the crop is cut. The cutter bar – a row of triangular shaped knives – is adjusted hydraulically, and some machines have flotation devices which enable the combine to follow the contours of a field.

And on the giant modern machines which cut the extensive cereal crops in the huge fields of East Anglia the operator doesn't steer by line of sight. He uses GPS satellite signals to ensure the combine follows an accurate course across the ground.

Transferring grain from combine to trailer

Combine header

Grass Cutting Machinery

Grass is the most important agricultural crop in the UK. A field of good quality grass may be cut three times a year to make silage or hay to feed cattle when they cannot graze outside.

Most agricultural mowers use a drum or disc to which are attached two or three swinging blades. Mowers are often mounted to the back and front of a tractor, and using two smaller mowers rather than one large one reduces the size of the swathe, which aids the dryng process

Mowers are mounted behind the tractor but to one side of it so they are cutting grass that has not been flattened by the tractor wheels.

Mower conditioner mowing grass

Conditioners

To make good silage, grass must be "scuffed" or conditioned to allow moisture to escape and the grass to dry more quickly. This is done by a mower attachment called a conditioner which is usually incorporated into the back of the cutting deck.

The stems of the cut grass are bruised to release the sap and speed the drying process before the grass is left on the ground.

Tedders

In haymaking newly-cut grass must be turned several times to expose it to the air, using machines called tedders, swathers or turners which toss the grass using rotating spikes. The grass is also laid into rows for collection.

Toppers

Pasture toppers are towed by tractor to take the 'top' off pasture, removing weeds like

Tedders or Spreaders turn the grass duriing haymaking

Topping grass

thistles and docks to stop them going to seed and spreading.

Toppers do not cut tight to the ground and are mounted straight behind the tractor as what they are cutting is not used as a crop so it doesn't matter if the farmer drives over it.

Hedge Cutters
In many parts of the country hedges form the principal boundaries between fields and these are normally cut back once a year.

Hedge trimming

Nowadays this is almost always done using a heavy-duty flail cutter attached to the rear of a tractor.

The cutting head is angled by hydraulic rams which enable the tops, sides and bottom of the hedge to be reached. The cutters can deal with small trees as well as hedges, and are also used to cut the sides of ditches and banks.

The flails spin on a rotor three thousand times a minute, although they run slower when grass cutting flails are attached to trim verges. Hedge cutters can use the tractor's hydraulic system or be powered independently.

Balers

Conventional baler

The huge quantities of grass that are cut in the summer to feed to animals in the winter as silage have to be stored. Most of it is collected by trailer and put into silage clamps in the farmyard.

But about a quarter of all silage is made into bales and stored in the farmyard, or kept in the fields close to where it will be needed for feeding. The swathes of grass are picked up by tractor-pulled baling machines which compact the grass into round, cylindrical or square bales and leave them in rows.

The machines tie the bales with string (baler twine) before discharging them, or wrap them with self-clinging plastic net. Many balers use blades to chop the grass into smaller pieces to help the fermentation process.

Straw and Hay are also baled but because making silage and haylage requires the grass to be stored in airtight conditions, only these bales are wrapped. A separate bale wrapper is normally used for this process, and big bales are wrapped in six layers of polythene film. Even with this protection birds, rats and mice do sometimes puncture the wrapper and once air gets into a bale it can be ruined.

Moving bales, particularly silage bales with their high moisture content, requires heavy duty machinery. A silage bale only five feet long can weigh half a ton.

This is why you will often see tractors or fork lift trucks with spikes or other big bale handling attachments moving bales from field to farmyard. Another way of moving large bales is with hydraulically-operated gripper arms.

Smaller bales can be fed into an "accumulator" – a sledge towed behind the baler which leaves them in a pattern suitable for collection later. Two rows of four bales side by side are known as a "flat eight," a formation suitable for collection by a bale grab on a tractor loader or forklift.

Buckrake

Wet grass is very heavy, so making silage requires heavy-duty machinery. Trailers bring the grass to the silage clamp, but it then has to be spread evenly and "squashed" to turn it into an anaerobic state.

The usual device for spreading silage is a buckrake, an attachment on the front or rear of a tractor with tines which lock upwards to hold and transport the grass and are released to tip it into the clamp.

Bale handler at front and spike at rear

Front end buckrake

The aim is to spread the silage evenly to help it compress and expel air. Once it is spread, the tractor runs over the silage again and again and the weight of the buckrake adds pressure to help this process.

The buckrake is sometimes attached to a four-wheel drive "handler" vehicle which has a telescopic ram to reach all the corners of the clamp and is used as an alternative to a tractor because it can can lift heavy weights much higher and for greater distances.

Forage Harvesters

Forage is a crop harvested to feed animals and it can be cereals, rape or vegetables. But the most important forage crop is grass for silage.

Forage harvesters pick up the grass from swathes left in a field, chop it into smaller pieces for better fermentation and blow it into a trailer. The harvester may be pulled by a tractor or it may be self-propelled.

There are different "headers" for each type of silage. Those that collect maize have large conical separators that pass between the rows of maize and force the crop back into the harvester. Maize harvesters have kernel processors or "corn crackers" - two mill rolls with teeth which are pressed together by springs.

Silage forager filling silage trailer

Many forage harvesters have built-in knife sharpening systems and most have means of detecting stray pieces of metal in a field and preventing damage to the blades.

Pea Viners

Specialist machines known as pea viners are needed to harvest the large acreage of peas

Pea viner

and broad beans grown for human consumption in the UK – most destined to be frozen. (Field peas and beans, an important food for animals, are cut by combine harvesters.)

The pea viners cut the vines, and a conveyor belt takes the vines and pods to a threshing drum, where the peas are removed. The empty pods and other waste material are returned to the ground for ploughing back into the field.

During the pea harvest, which runs from mid June until September, depending on the locality of the farm, pea viners usually work in convoy around the clock to ensure the crop is harvested in ideal conditions – there is an eight hour window when the peas are at their best.

Driers

If harvested grain is too wet it will turn mouldy and have to be thrown away. To be stored safely for long periods wheat, barley and oats must have a moisture content of no more than 14%, and when it is harvested it may have as much as 25% moisture.

The moisture content can be reduced either by blowing warm air through it when it is stored in a grain store or bin, or by putting it in a high temperature drier before storage.

The most common type of drier is a tower with two fans and a heater. Damp grain drops slowly through the tower and hot air is blown through the perforated sides. As it falls to the bottom the grain is then cooled in the same way, this time with unheated air.

The high temperature drier uses the same principle, but this time the unit is horizontal and the grain is moved through the drier on a conveyor belt.

When grain is stored some distance from the main farm buildings, a portable grain drier is often used.

Mixers and Feeders

Additional feed has to be given to livestock, especially over the winter, and most farms have machinery to mill, mix and deliver food to animals, usually in the farmyard. The larger mills and mixers are permanently housed in farm buildings – hidden away from public gaze.

But mobile units, powered by the tractor, are used to chop and mix straw, silage and hay with other ingredients such as molasses or food concentrates. The food is mixed in a hopper and fed by conveyor to feeding troughs.

Large bales are convenient for storage, but they need to be broken up before being given to livestock. Mobile choppers cut up the bales and blow the chopped straw up to twenty metres into cattle pens. Hay and silage can be treated in the same way,

Feed mixer

Rollers

Most crops need to be planted in a field that is level and smooth. Harrows and cultivators may break up the clods left by ploughing, but by themselves they will not leave a satisfactory seedbed.

Rolling prepared ground

Farmers use rollers to finish the job. "Cambridge" rollers have ribbed wheels which are more effective than smooth rollers in crushing clods and breaking up the soil.

"Crumbler" rollers are an open cage with steel rods which achieve the same effect, with the weight concentrated on the lower rod to add maximum pressure. Heavier versions are called packer rollers.

A Furrow Press is usually attached to the back of a plough and uses large iron wheels

Cambridge roller

to level out the furrows as soon as the plough has created them. Lightweight rollers are also used after seeds have been drilled to make sure the ground is compacted and seeds make good contact with the soil to aid germination.

Grassland has to be rolled early in the summer if it has stones or other bumps in the ground which might make it difficult for mowers to cut silage and hay later in the season. Heavier rollers are needed for this task and these are often hollow cylinders which are filled with water or other ballast to increase pressure.

Sprayers

Most crops need to be protected against weeds, insects and diseases, and a wide range of sprayers are used. "Wide" is the correct term, because many sprayers have booms extending for forty metres to enable large areas to be sprayed quickly.

Many sprayers have wide booms

Sprayers may be self-propelled or trailed behind a tractor and the acreage that can be sprayed in one trip is determined by the size of the tank and the concentration of the chemical being used.

Very low applications of pesticides and herbicides are becoming more common, and these are sometimes delivered through rotary atomisers rather than normal spray nozzles.

To avoid waste, some crop sprayers apply chemicals in narrow bands instead of right across the field, especially when treating the ground before planting vegetables.

Irrigation

Many crops need additional water to flourish, even in the damp UK climate. This is particularly true of potatoes, sugar beet and vegetables grown on a large scale. Light soils in the drier eastern side of the country – where these crops are most common – are in particular need of irrigation.

Portable or semi-permanent pipelines, usually made of aluminium, carry water from reservoirs, rivers or boreholes to the field, where rotating sprinklers with spring loaded nozzles distribute the water through 360 degrees.

A cheaper alternative is the use of self-propelled mobile irrigators: wheeled trolleys which carry a large reel of hose attached to a rain gun. The reel is attached to a water supply at the side of a field and the trolley is towed across to the other side of the field to unwind the hose.

Once irrigation begins, a turbine, driven by the water, rewinds the hose, which pulls the trolley slowly back across the field. As it moves, water is pumped to the rain gun or sprinkler.

Mobile irrigation trolley

Loaders

One of the most common tractor attachments is a front loader used for carrying bulk materials such as grain, fertilisers and straw bales to and from different parts of the farm.

The frame of the loader is attached to the tractor behind the front wheels and two heavy-duty arms pivot at the front end of the frame. The loader is raised by two rams powered by the tractor's hydraulic system.

Different buckets, forks and grabs are used to pick up or deposit root vegetables, pallets, silage, fertiliser bags and bales of different sizes.

Post Driver

Fences on farms have to be repaired and replaced on a regular basis, and strong posts are the basis of any fencing system. To be rigid and long-lasting, posts must be firmly established in the ground and this is normally done with the aid of machines which are attached to a tractor and use its hydraulic power to operate an iron or steel hammer.

The post is held in position while the hammer drives it into the ground. Post drivers sometimes have additional equipment such as rockspikes for very hard ground, or excavator attachments. Heaver versions may be attached to a front loader.

Spreaders

To help crops to grow, nutrients in the form of manure, minerals and fertiliser must be added to the ground. Because the material comes in different forms, a range of machinery has been devised which uses paddles, flails, pumps and discs to spread it evenly from tanks and trailers.

Slurry, or liquid manure, is sucked or top filled into a tanker from the slurry lagoon. Vacuum tankers are pressurised and the slurry expelled from the rear by a deflector plate, or sprayed from the top of the tank with a slurry gun.

Other spreaders are emptied by gravity and the slurry is spread by a disc spinning under the outlet.

Slurry spreader

Post driver

Spreading fertiliser

Growing environmental concerns about the leaching of nitrate from the soil have led to restrictions on the amount of slurry that can be applied to the land, especially in dairy farming areas where there are large amounts of animal waste to dispose of. To apply the slurry more precisely, it is often injected into the soil using frame-mounted tines on the back of the slurry tank.

Spreading chains inside dung spreader

Solid farmyard manure (dung) has to be broken up before it can be applied to the field. This is done by manure spreaders with rotary blades or beaters before being spread by flails from the side or rear of the vehicles.

Fertiliser is much easier to spread because it normally comes as powder or granules. It is applied using "broadcasters" which have one or two horizontal stainless steel discs which receive the fertiliser from a hopper and spread it evenly over a wide area. Sometimes an oscillating spout is used instead of a disc.

Trailed broadcasters are also used to spread lime on fields in the autumn.

Where more precision is needed in the application of fertiliser – matching the tramlines in large cereal fields, for example – pneumatic distributors using long booms similar to crop sprayers may be used.

Dung spreading

Wildlife and the Farmer

The British Isles are blessed with a wide range of rich and diverse habitats which house an even larger array of wildlife. The landscape that we see today - the homes, territories and environments of our wildlife - have been shaped over many thousands of years by our need to produce food and find places to live.

In this chapter we explore the wildlife behind the hedge, see how farming has affected our wildlife and, in turn, how wildlife affects our farming.

The term wildlife refers to animals and plants which are not cultivated or domesticated. The animals we have looked at earlier are farmed: they are here because people tend them, just as the animals we keep as pets are not wildlife.

In Britain we have species which are native. They have been here for thousands of years and arrived without introduction by humans. Foxes are a good example. We also have species which are naturalised. They have been introduced to our country from

A fox cub hiding in a hedge

different places in the world, but have learned to live in the environments they find themselves without needing human care.

Classic examples of naturalised species are rabbits and pheasants which are believed to have been introduced to Britain by the Normans at the beginning of the twelfth century.

Wild Rabbit in a farmyard

Cock Pheasants sparring

Farming and Wildlife

The huge changes that have taken place in British farming during the last two hundred years have had a big impact upon our wildlife. A brief look at how the landscape of farming has altered is necessary for any exploration into wildlife behind the hedge today.

The Industrial Revolution turned Britain into the first truly urban nation. The growth of first canals, then railways and finally new roads helped towns to grow rapidly; large towns meant more people and more food needed to feed them. Improved transport also made it easier to import food from outside the United Kingdom.

These developments led to the British countryside, its wildlife and the farmer's ways of working becoming strange and distant to much of the population of Britain.

Technological advances also brought new machinery: drills, reaping and threshing machines, tractors and later the combine harvester. Production costs were lowered whilst crop yields increased. The land was being used much more intensively.

This progress was disrupted in the 1870s when bad harvests and increased food imports led to the Agricultural Depression,

Hard times in the 1890s

Hedges grubbed out to make larger fields

which lasted roughly thirty years. Farming families who had worked in and with the countryside and its wildlife all their lives moved away.

The nineteenth century also saw changes in woodland management. Much of Britain's native woodland was cleared to create softwood forests and larger areas for farming. Hedgerows, which had only been in place for a short time when the countryside was being enclosed some hundred years or so before, were ripped out to create larger fields.

The post-war period of the twentieth century saw the drive for efficiency and increased yields continue especially with food rationing still in mind. Labour was also in short supply so farms became more mechanised with bigger fields to accommodate the new machinery. The factor which had the greatest impact upon our wildlife at this time was the enhanced use of pesticides and fertilizers, driven by Government and the large companies supplying them.

Farmers are responsible for looking after seventy five per cent of Britain's landscape, and have a duty of care for the land and its features, the homes and habitats of our wildlife.

In recent years we have come to recognise this duty of care for our countryside, for the natural world and all that lives in it; we are beginning to understand how to work with nature to enhance our environment and wildlife. Life is a cycle - what comes from the earth goes back to the earth - and all plants and animals play a part in this sequence.

Losing any part of this cycle has a big knock-on effect on the complex web of tendrils that holds our environment together, whether this is part of the food chain or, as in the case of bees, an essential part of the pollination process.

Honey bee on dandelion

We now realise that farming is important to our wildlife and needs to be undertaken with care. If farmers stopped managing the countryside, trees would soon take over the landscape and dominant plants such as brambles, bracken, stinging nettles, thistles and docks would run riot. Just look what happens to a neglected garden.

A Delicate Balance with Soil and Disease

If you were to step outside and scoop up a teaspoon's worth of earth, you would be holding in your hand approximately five billion living organisms. This healthy, fertile, nutrient rich soil is, of course, the basis for our living world: our wildlife and our farming is wholly dependent upon the wellbeing of the soil.

The organisms, vitamins and minerals within the soil are essential for life above the ground. So, for example, the long-time growing of monocultures (i.e. one variety such as rye grass) across a vast expanse of land (as opposed to meadowland which may have upwards of fifty different varieties of plant species) will progressively deplete the earth of its natural nutrients. This can then lead to mass soil erosion.

The depletion of these nutrients also means that grassland or crops are not nutrient rich, and this loss of essential vitamins and minerals continues up through the food chain. Animals grazing or feeding upon depleted grass or crops are not getting the nutrients they need, which of course means that humans do not get them either. The use of pesticides and fertilizers further unbalances the natural state of the soil.

However in order to grow the food we need, farmers themselves are faced with a range of natural crop diseases and pests which have to be avoided or controlled. The diseases fall into four categories: seed-borne, air-borne, vector-borne and soil-borne.

Seed-borne diseases have become much rarer due to seed treatments such as fungicides before planting. In the UK we have Seed Certification Schemes which ensure healthy seed is planted.

Air-borne diseases are of fungal or bacterial origin and the spores are dispersed by the wind or air currents. In the right environmental conditions they can destroy

Monoculture: a field of rye grass

Meadow with a range of wild flowers

a crop rapidly. Potato blight, yellow rusts of wheat and barley and canker in all brassicas and oilseed rape fall into this category.

Crop rotation does not control these diseases and farmers try to use resistant varieties, or several different ones, to avoid spraying which is very costly. The cost of treatment must be set against the value of the crop: is it viable to treat?

Vector-borne diseases of importance are carried by Aphids or Nematodes (vectors are carriers of disease) and are all viruses. Infection often occurs with early sown autumn and late sown spring crops, when aphids are very active. Specific sprays are used to target the vectors.

Feral pigeon

Snail

Aphid

Soil-borne diseases have limited mobility. For example, resting spores can survive for years until a susceptible host plant comes along. Leeks and onions are affected by the fungus Smut which can survive dormant for ten years and White Rot for eight years. It can be carried from field to field on machinery or boots so if plants are infected they must be burnt and not ploughed back in to the soil. Chemical control is very difficult, expensive and rarely used, so either a resistant variety of a crop is planted or a different cropping sequence used.

Crops are attacked by many animal pests including insects, slugs, snails, mites, birds (pigeon) and mammals (Fallow Deer) and there are strict codes of practice for their controls. With growing concern over the use of chemical control, smaller quantities are used in a more selective manner.

The England Rural Development Programme (ERDP) was set up to ensure farming in the UK was sustainable and environmentally responsible. Farmers and foresters are given grants to encourage them to adopt agricultural methods which benefit our wildlife and historic environment.

Among the most important of these government schemes is the Environmental Stewardship Scheme, the aims of which include the encouragement of biodiversity, the conservation of wildlife, better public understanding of and access to the countryside, and improved flood management.

Linking Environment and Farming (LEAF) is an organisation designed to promote environmentally responsible farming. Its members host visits by the public on Open Farm Sunday once a year and allow their farms to be used to demonstrate best practice. If they meet the highest standards of sustainability their products are able to carry the LEAF marque, a valuable marketing tool.

The Farming and Wildlife Advisory Group (FWAG) is a national charity which aims to assist farmers and landowners in the conservation of our natural and historic environment. Like LEAF, the charity offers farmers advice on how best to manage their land in a way which is both productive and improves the natural environment.

Wildlife behind the Hedge

Habitats differ from one type of farming to another, and so does the wildlife they support. This chapter is not a definitive list of all the plants, trees, birds, fungi and animals found on farmland. It seeks to illustrate how changing farming practice and

man have depleted the ecosystems which are needed to sustain different species of wildlife and how farmers and conservationists are re-establishing sensitive habitats.

Fungi are a diverse and huge family of organisms which occur in different and often beautiful guises in many habitats. Unlike plants they cannot produce their own food so they absorb nutrients from their surroundings and process dead plant material and animal matter through decay. For example they help turn a cow pat into soil. The string-like filaments of fungi

Bracket Fungi

Fly Agaric

which exist amongst the roots of plants help to pass on essential nutrients to the plants, without which they could not grow.

Many types of fungus can be eaten and it is also used to make bread, blue cheeses and beer. Penicillin comes from a fungus and saves live by killing harmful bacteria.

Water Vole

Rivers, Streams, Ditches

Moving water, whether it is a fast-running river or a trickling brook, provides habitats, spawning and mating sites and feeding grounds for many different plant and animal species. Fish, amphibians (tadpole), eels, dragonflies and damselflies are among the more obvious examples, but these waterways are also home to rarer mammals such as the water vole and otter.

Marsh Marigold

Rivers, streams and ditches are teaming with invertebrates such as mayflies and beetles, whilst plants like reed grasses, yellow iris, marsh marigold, and water forget-me-not are specially adapted to watery life. The blue flash of the kingfisher as it dives for its supper, and the long legs of the grey heron wading into the water, alert us to the bird life a river or stream supports. Swans and cormorants are found near larger rivers and Canada geese regularly on inland ponds.

Otter

On the farm these watercourses provide drinking water for cattle and other stock, but if too many animals have access to a long stretch of water, riverbanks can collapse and soil can be eroded. This can be managed if livestock can only access parts of the water. This will prevent banks collapsing and allow plants to flourish.

Apart from industrial pollution the main environmental danger to our rivers and streams in recent years has been pollution

Damselfly

from the farm. This comes in many forms and includes pesticides and fertilizers as well as accidental spills of milk, silage and slurry (undiluted animal manure).

These are all extremely harmful to the life of our waterways. Bacteria (crypto-sporidium) from slurry and chemicals from pesticides lead to the death of many water species, whilst fertilizers and slurry contain phosphates and nitrates which are polluting in large quantities.

These allow algae to cover the water surface and rob the river of its oxygen, causing the death of fish, invertebrates and plants. In

Hungry Kingfisher

turn, this deprives birds and mammals of a valuable source of food.

Ponds

Ponds on the farm can be permanent or temporary (the ones that dry out at certain times of the year) and both are important to our wildlife. Temporary ponds have become a threatened habitat as they are often converted into permanent ponds, or discarded altogether by infilling.

The pond habitat does not finish at the edge of the water, but continues beyond the pond margins. Ponds provide homes for amphibians such as frogs and newts, feeding grounds for birds and mammals, and places

Swan incubating eggs

Pond covered in algae

Coot feeding its young

for invertebrates to lay their eggs (dragonflies and damselflies, for example). Ponds also play host to a vast number of wetland plants, such as water starwort which changes its appearance depending on the flow and depth of the water where the plant grows. As with rivers, streams and ditches, the biggest problem with ponds on farms is avoiding pollution; excessive algae and duckweed coverage caused by increased nutrients suffocates the life within the pond. The introduction of non-native plants such as the Himalayan Balsam, a garden escapee, can have the same affect.

Frogs and Newts

Awareness of the importance of ponds to our wildlife is the first step towards best practice. Vegetation should be allowed to grow up around the margins of ponds, whilst animals should be restricted to certain areas of the pond edge if no other drinking water is available. Increasingly farmers with main water supplies to their fields are fencing off ponds to allow the natural habitat to regenerate. When they are spreading manure, slurry or chemical fertilizers, farmers now keep it well away from watercourses.

Woodland

In Britain we have deciduous woodlands and conifer woodlands. Deciduous woodland is made up of trees which, for the most part,

Water Starwort

lose their leaves every year in the autumn before re-growing them each spring. The types of trees within our deciduous woodlands may vary in different parts of the country, though species such as oak, beech, ash, hazel, hornbeam, blackthorn and hawthorn are the most plentiful.

Woodland does not have to cover acres of land in order to be a wonderful wildlife habitat. On many farms small pockets of woodland provide homes for a wide variety of different plant and animal species.

One of the joys of spring is to stumble across a piece of woodland carpeted in bluebells, wood anemone, wood sorrel, lungwort, lesser celandine, wild garlic and freshly emerging ferns. Woodlands are also home to some of our rarer plants such as the purple orchid, herb paris and yellow archangel and they provide excellent sites for the many types of fungi, lichen and moss in the British Isles.

The bird population of our deciduous woodlands may vary from place to place, but the tit family is known to most of us. A stroll through a piece of woodland may also enable us to see bullfinches, nuthatches, tree creepers, woodcock, woodpeckers, jays,

Himalayan Balsam

Conservation pond on a farm

Wild garlic in deciduous woodland

rooks, siskin, sparrow hawks and tawny owls.

These are some of the birds that use the trees not merely to nest in, but also to search for food. Mammals such as the wood mouse, dormouse and yellow-necked mouse live beneath the canopied layers, whilst slugs, snails and beetles inhabit the woodland floor.

Larger mammals such as roe deer, badger and foxes are found in woodlands, and so are the speckled wood, orange tip and comma butterflies. We may even be lucky enough to catch a glimpse of the rare Heath Fritillary, the Glanville Fritillary and the Small Copper, in addition to over three hundred different varieties of moth.

Over the past two centuries we have seen woodlands cleared to make room for larger fields and the planting of conifer trees (see

below) which has had the effect of destroying not only the ancient trees but also the plant and animal life within.

Woodland on the farm can provide shelter for livestock and game birds as well as providing an income from timber, if

Beech masts

managed correctly. As with hedgerows, a sensible margin should be left around the edges of pieces of woodland, whilst the practice of coppicing in some areas may greatly benefit wildlife.

Coppicing allows light to filter in through the canopy of the woodland, ensuring that plants

do not live in wholly shady areas and can thrive. These provide shelter and sustenance for many invertebrates, mammals, birds and insects, which in turn may become food for larger species.

Lichen and moss

Herb Paris

Bluebell wood

Blue Tit

Wood Mice in a grain store

Siskin

Bloody Nosed Beatle

Sparrow Hawk

In Britain we have two distinct types of conifer woodland: the native conifer woodland - which today can only be found in the highlands of Scotland and is known as Caledonian Forest - and the plantation forests. The native conifer woodlands are primarily made up of Scots Pine, birch, alder, juniper, rowan, bird cherry, eared willow, hazel, holly, oak and aspen - providing a rich ecosystem.

Plant and animal species particular to this specialised habitat may include the pine marten, wild cat, red squirrel, Scottish crossbill, cowberry and twinflower.

Imported species such as larch (deciduous), Douglas Fir and Sitka Spruce are the varieties

Small Copper butterfly

Glanville Fritillary butterfly

most commonly found in our plantation woodlands. These woodlands are usually planted for timber. They may grow up to six times faster than broad-leafed trees, and thus make more efficient and profitable use of a piece of land.

Until recently conifers were planted very close together, which allowed little or no light to reach the forest floor, whilst the thick carpet of needles building up on the ground means that very few plants can survive. With few plant species, the variety of wildlife of these conifer forests is much less than that of our deciduous woodland. However, we do see many varieties of fungi and birds such as the chaffinch, coal tit and goshawk making conifer woodlands their home.

Today there is a large emphasis upon the conservation of our woodlands, and the protection of native trees as opposed to species introduced and rapidly planted during the mid twentieth century. Where plantations occur more care is taken to ensure that they are designed with conservation in mind; areas

Caledonian woodland

Pine Marten

Wild Cat

Plantation forest

are set aside for deciduous planting, whilst tracks or rides are left unplanted to connect areas of natural plant life.

Farm Buildings

When we look behind the hedge and see beautiful old stone or slate farm buildings, we may appreciate them for their beauty, or as a reminder of times gone by. We may also look upon newer or dilapidated structures as unsightly and consider the remains of old barns to be taking up vital space or becoming a hazard to people and animals.

However, these structures, whether standing or tumbled down, are one of the best habitats for wildlife. They provide a range of perfect roosting and nesting sites for an array of birds such as the barn owl, swallow, house martin, swift and house sparrow; and bat species like the pipistrelle, natterer's bat and daubenton's bat.

Derelict barns provide ideal wildlife habitats

Barn Owl

Other farm buildings have been converted into houses or demolished for development leading to a loss of habitat for particular sections of our wildlife. But wildlife is infinitely adaptable, and even modern farm buildings have been taken over by a host of birds and bats.

One species is not very welcome: rats. Larger farms with bigger storage areas for grain or animal feed mean larger communities of rats can be supported. Rats carry a host of diseases and grain storage barns and bins have to be made as vermin proof as possible.

It is not only the buildings which provide homes for our wildlife, but also the area surrounding farm buildings, particularly those which are no longer in use and have a thick cover of vegetation. This creates another distinct habitat, supplying birds and bats with food and nesting materials.

There is of course a silver lining to this cloud, as rats are scavengers and play their part in our rural life cycle. They also provide a tasty meal for a number of other animals such as birds of prey and snakes.

Over recent years farm buildings in Britain have reduced in number partly because farms are now much larger, and so fewer buildings may be needed, but also because old style barns and animal housing have changed to make way for newer designs (which may not include the eaves, beams and roof spaces of older buildings).

Grassland

In Britain grassland is primarily the result of the clearance of woodland which has taken place throughout the past few thousand years. Today much of our agricultural landscape is dominated by land which has been 'improved' for grazing or for the production of crops by seeding.

Crows now nest in disused dovecotes

Areas which are predominantly used to grow one particular crop (monoculture), or are grazed intensively, have a much smaller range of plant and animal life. Although now, all over the country, wider margins are being left at the edges of fields as conservation strips and some are planted with wild flower mixes. The field poppy is now seen less often in a field of corn because farmers don't wish to combine poppies with their grain, although it is widespread in field margins and on wasteland.

Different types of grassland in different parts of the country play host to a mixture of wildlife depending upon the soil type and geographical location. In many areas we are still blessed with unimproved grassland (land which has not been ploughed, fertilised or reseeded) and meadows which are rich in wildflowers and provide habitats and food for many mammals, birds and insects.

A meadow full of wildflowers and grasses is one of the joys of summer, bursting with colour, smells, and the sounds of a thousand insects drinking in the sweet nectar. Oxeye daisy, knapweed, clover, buttercup, thistles, harebells, vetch, snake's head fritillary and orchids are some of the treasures to be found.

Butterflies such as the common blue, pale clouded yellow and meadow brown are

Grass Snake

Meadow Brown

Poppies in a cornfield

Tufted Vetch

Common Orchid

livestock, whilst at the same time encouraging biodiversity. Grazing is an important part of the management of wildlife, as grazing helps to suppress the re-emergence of scrub and woodland on areas where it is unwanted.

Hedgerows

The hedgerows of Britain support a wide range of plants and animals, yet since the mid twentieth century we have seen a dramatic loss of hedges on Britain's farms. Between 1984 and 1990 nearly a quarter of the length of our hedgerows was destroyed. This loss includes some of those ancient hedgerows which existed prior to the Enclosures Acts (1720-1840) as well as those more recently established.

resplendent amongst the grass and flowers. All manner of mammals and birds are dependent upon our grasslands and, as always, live within a delicately-balanced ecosystem.

Attempts are now being made to apply different methods of farming the land which will be kinder to our wildlife without limiting the ability to produce efficiently and effectively. Conservation Grazing is one such initiative which aims to use grazing animals to manage sites of conservation interest.

Farmers are supported as they try to find the right grazing regime to suit their

Birds nest in a hawthorn bush

A pair of badgers

Weasel

Hedgerows not only provide homes and feeding sites for small mammals such as weasels, hedgehogs and mice but also for a wealth of insects and birds. And they act as passageways between different habitats for a number of species such as foxes and badgers.

The most popular plant in the British hedgerow is hawthorn: it provides a thick and impenetrable mass of thorny branches perfect for enclosing livestock. Holly and the rarer butchers broom are two of the few non-deciduous plants that makes up the hedgerow. Other common species include hazel, dogwood, elder, spindle, rowan, blackthorn and crab apple.

Hedgerow flowers

Most hedges also sustain an enormous selection of smaller plants, including climbers such as honeysuckle and ivy. One of the most beautiful visions of our countryside is the hedgerow in full bloom: foxgloves mingle with red campion, stitchwort, violets, bluebell, wild strawberries, toadflax and primroses.

Aside from the abundance of flora and fauna in our hedgerows, they are also important features of our agricultural landscape. Not

Spindle

only do they act as boundaries and enclose livestock, they are also crucial to maintaining topsoil in windy areas. In parts of the country where hedges have been grubbed out to create very large fields - East Anglia, for example - wind erosion is a perpetual problem.

Nowadays farmers are encouraged to manage hedgerows by coppicing, laying, trimming and cutting at appropriate times of the year and a ten metre margin from the base of the hedge is left clear when using agricultural machinery such as balers or harvesters.

Rabbit burrows undermining a hedge

Our landscape is the product of thousands of years of man-made change, and our wildlife has had to adapt to these constant changes. Farming, which is largely responsible for the natural world behind the hedge, can benefit from a wider understanding of the delicate balance of our wildlife, for example the need for crop rotation or the maintenance of healthy soil, and there is every indication that many farmers are becoming champions of a more sustainable and varied countryside.

Mr Fox has the last word

Glossary of Terms

Abattoir Also known as a slaughterhouse; where animals are killed and carcass preparation takes place

Acre The traditional unit of land area of one chain long and one furlong wide, or 4840 square yards

AI Artificial Insemination

Arable Farming The growing of crops in fields on ploughed land

Ark A mobile pig or poultry house commonly made of corrugated iron

Auroch A wild ox, now extinct

Baconer A pig reared for bacon

Baling Compressing hay or straw into round or square bales to be used for food or bedding

Bantam Very small breeds of hens and other fowl

Beef The meat of cattle but not of calves

Billets Chopped lengths of wood

Billy Male goat

Biofuel Fuels such as ethanol produced from plants and other organic matter

Biomass Organic matter such as willow or miscanthus used to produce energy

Blanch To keep plant stalks white by covering them up (e.g. celery and asparagus)

Blow Fly Strike When the blow fly lays its eggs on the fleece of a sheep

Boar An un-castrated male pig

Boning Removing the meat from the bones of a carcass

Bovine Relating to cattle

Break Crop One grown between regular planting of another crop, often a cereal, to improve the soil

Brindle Tawny or brownish with streaks of other colours

Bristles A pig's hairs

Broadcast Historic (and wasteful) way of spreading seed by hand

Broiler A chicken, usually less than three months old, reared for meat

Brome A common weed which affects cereals (often called barren or sterile brome)

Brooder Heat provided by a lamp or gas to keep chicks warm

Brucellosis Infectious disease of livestock which can be transmitted to humans

Buck Male rabbit, goat or deer

Buffer Feeding Providing additional food to livestock when grazing is inadequate

Bulk Tank Chilled stainless steel tank for holding milk

Bull Un-castrated male cattle

Bull Beef Un-castrated males that are reared to meat weight very quickly before the fact that they are male has chance to taint the flavour of the meat

Bullock Castrated bull or young bull

Cake Pelleted feed usually made from a mix of cereals and minerals

Calf Young cattle up to the age of weaning

Carcase/Carcass The body of an animal once it has been killed for meat

Castration Removing or making the testes of a young male animal dysfunctional, so it is unable to breed. It also makes the animal quieter to handle.

Catch Crop Fast growing crop sown between two main crops

Chick Young bird especially of domestic fowl

Chocolate Spot A disease affecting field beans

Clamp A pile of root crops such as potatoes covered with earth and straw to preserve them. A silage clamp preserves cut grass in anaerobic conditions with layers of polythene to keep out the air.

Clostridial diseases A group of anaerobic spore forming organisms found in the environment which produce fatal diseases such as blackleg, braxy and dysentery

Cluster A group of cups which fit over an animal's teats to extract milk

Coccidiosis A disease caused by single-cell microscopic organisms called coccidian.

Colostrum The first milk of an animal which is full of antibodies

Colt A young male horse

Combine Harvester A giant machine that cuts and threshes cereal crops in one continuous process, leaving straw in the field and grain in the trailer

Commoner A person whose has rights over a common piece of land

Common Land Land that is owned by somebody but over which another person has rights of use

Coppice An area of wood regularly cut back to enable new shoots to grow

Coulter The vertical cutting blade on a plough

Cover Crop A crop sown to prevent soil damage, or to provide cover for game birds

Creep Feeding Allowing young animals such as lambs or piglets to access food by using an entrance which is too small for larger animals to enter

Crisping Potatoes grown to make crisps

Cruck Wooden 'A' frames used in the construction of barns and other farm buildings

Cubicles Individual partitions in a cattle shed for cows to lie down

Cucurbit Melons, marrows and other members of the family cucurbitaceae

Cud Food that cows bring back from their first stomach to chew again

Cull To kill unwanted animals to keep populations under control or when controlling the spread of disease

Curd The part of the milk used to make cheese

Curds The flower heads of cauliflowers and broccoli

Curing Treating meat and skins to preserve them

Cutter A pig that weighs over 80 kilograms and is more than 150 days old

Dagging Cutting or shearing soiled areas of an animal's rump

Dairy The building where milk is processed or stored

Deadweight What a carcass weighs when it has been prepared or dressed

Dewlap Fold of loose skin hanging from animal's throat

Disbud Remove horn buds from a young animal

Dished Refers to the concave profile of an animal's face

Docking Removing the lower part of an animal's tail

Doe Female rabbit, goat or deer

Dosing see drenching

Double Muscling Increasing the fibres in muscle and so reducing the fat and connective tissue content

Draft Older ewe moved to lowland for breeding

Drenching To administer medication orally

Dressing Making a carcass fit for human consumption by cleaning it and removing the internal organs

Draught Animals used to pull heavy loads

Drill An implement used to sow seeds also the furrow in which they are sown

Drove A group of animals being driven

Drovers The person who moves the drove

Dried Off When an animal is no longer lactating

Duckling Young duck

Dun Greyish brown colour

Durum High-protein, hard grained variety of wheat preferred for pasta production

Entire An animal that still has its testicles, and can be used for breeding

Ewe A female sheep which has had a lamb

Fallow Fields left unplanted to allow the soil to recover its fertility

Farrow/Farrowing To give birth to piglets

Fatstock Livestock that is fat and ready for market

Fawn A young deer under a year of age

Feed Conversion Ratio The amount of feed required in kilograms to make an animal gain 1kg in weight

Fertiliser Any substance used to make soil more fertile

Field System A collection of fields

Filly A young female horse

Finching A coloured line or stripe running along the backbone of cattle

Finish To feed cattle and sheep until they are ready for slaughter

Flail Tool used to thresh (beat) cereals to extract the grain

Flock A group of sheep

Fodder beet Sugar beet grown for feeding to animals

Fold To keep animals in a restricted area; also the name for a group of Highland cattle

Foldyard Part of a farmyard used to keep and feed cattle in the winter

Foot and Mouth Disease A highly contagious disease of cloven hooved animals

Foot Rot A disease affecting the feet of any cloven hoofed animal

Forage Crops that animals can eat stored or in the field

Fowl Birds farmed for food

Fungicide A chemical used to control or kill fungi in crops

Furlong One eighth of a mile, or 220 yards. Traditionally it was the length of a furrow or the distance a team of oxen could plough without resting

Furrow Trench cut by a plough

Game Animals hunted for sport and food

Gander Male goose

Gelding A male animal which has been castrated, particularly a horse

Gilt A young female pig before she has her first litter

Gimmer A young female sheep which has been weaned but not yet sheared (approx 6 to 15mths old)

Glean Collect the remnants of crops after harvesting

Go Back When an animal loses condition

Goatling A female goat between the age of one and two years which has not had kids

Gosling Young goose

Green Manure Plants grown to plough back into the soil and enrich it

Grist Grain for milling

Harrow A device to break down the soil after ploughing and create a seedbed

Haulm Stalks of potatoes, peas and beans. Sometimes used as straw

Hay Long grass which is cut and dried in the summer to feed to animals in the winter

Haycock The traditional way of storing hay in circular mounds

Hectare Ten thousand square metres or 2.47 acres

Heft Group of highland sheep which keep to same area

Heifer Young female cattle that have not had a calf

Herbage Grass and other green plants eaten by grazing animals

Herbicide A chemical agent that either destroys plants or inhibits their growth

Herd A group of cattle, goats or deer

Herd Book Record of pedigree animals of a particular breed

Hide The removed skin of an animal

Hind A female deer

Hoe Implement for weeding

Hogg/Hoggett A sheep between six and twelve

months old

Husbandry The art of caring for animals

Hybrid The offspring of genetically different parents

Hydroponics Growing plants without soil, normally in a liquid solution

In Calf A cow or heifer when pregnant

In Kid A female goat when pregnant

In Lamb A ewe when pregnant

Insecticide Chemical substance used to destroy insects

Keep Land rented for grazing

Keet Young Guinea Fowl

Kid Young goat

Killing out percentage The proportion of an animal that is edible

Kitten Young rabbit (or cat)

Knacker Man Someone who humanely kills and disposes of sick or dead animals

Lactation Production of milk

Lairage Part of an abattoir where animals are rested or held until slaughter

Lamb Young sheep

Lanolin Grease from sheep's wool used to make soap, etc

Leach Wash out of the soil

Ley An arable field temporarily under grass as part of a rotational system

Less Favoured Area (LFA) An area with natural disadvantages such as lack of water, or land that is mountainous or hilly

Linhay A two storey shelter for cattle with a hay loft above

Litter Group of mammals born to mother at same time; animal bedding

Liveweight The weight of a live animal

Loam Dark fertile soil which crumbles easily

Lodging When crops bend and lie flat to the ground, making machine harvesting difficult

Lop Ears Ears that hang forward to the sides of an animal's face, especially pig

Maiden Gilt A female pig over 6 months of age which has not yet been mated

Marbling The fat found between the muscles in meat

Marl Crumbling sedimentary rock also known as clayey limestone used as fertiliser

Mastitis Inflammation and infection of the udder

Meal A dry mix of feed ingredients

Midden A dunghill/heap or a term to describe an old rubbish heap

Milking parlour A place where cows or other animals are milked

Minimum tillage Shallow cultivation of the soil instead of deep ploughing

Monoculture The cultivation of a single crop

Mouldboard The part of a plough which turns the earth and makes the furrow

Mule Offspring of donkey and horse; crossbred sheep from a Blue-Faced Leicester Ram and hill ewes

Mutton The meat of a mature sheep

Muzzle Nose and mouth of an animal

Nanny Female goat

Nitrate Sensitive Areas Where restrictions on nitrate use on farm land are in force to reduce water contamination

Nurse Crop Grown to protect another crop and allow it to establish

Offal There are two kinds of offal; red offal which you can eat such as the liver, kidneys and heart and green offal which is the digestive tract and lungs

Out-wintered Animals that are hardy enough to be kept outdoors in the winter

Over-wintering Sending sheep from upland to less harsh lowland areas for the winter

Ovine Referring to sheep

Pasteurisation Heating to a specific temperature to destroy harmful bacteria

Pedigree Crops and Livestock from long-established breeding lines

Perennial Plants which grow for longer than two years

Permanent Pasture Grazed land that is not normally ploughed

Pesticide A chemical used to kill pests such as insects or rodents

Piglet A young pig

Pitchfork A pole with a forked end used to toss hay or bedding

Ploughshare The heavy blade of a plough

Poach Catch animals illegally; also to trample farmland in wet weather

Points The different coloured coat markings usually on the tips of the ears, muzzle etc. of an animal

Poll To dehorn an animal

Polled An animal that is naturally hornless

Pollination When the male pollen grain is introduced to the female part of a flower to fertilise it

Polytunnel Plastic greenhouse

Porker A pig reared for fresh meat rather than bacon

Poult Young fowl

Poultry Domestic birds kept for meat and eggs

Pullet Hen under a year old

Quota – milk Limit to the amount of milk produced

Race Hurdles arranged with a narrow passage for easy handling of sheep

Raddle Dye either smeared on the chest of a ram or in a dye block on a harness attached to the male animal that leaves a mark on the female's rump to show that

she has been mated

Rare Breed Park A farm that is dedicated to conserving rare species of animals

Ram An entire male sheep

Reap To cut crops such as wheat, barley, rye and oats

Replacement Heifers which replace ageing cows in a dairy herd

Rhizome Plant stems that grow under the ground

Rip Break up the soil

Roan Animal's coat in which a dark colour is sprinkled with white hairs

Rough Grazing Unimproved grassland on moor lands and uplands

Ruminant Animal such as a cow with several compartments in its stomach which help it to digest grass and other fibrous foods

Run Off The residue of fertilisers and pesticides which can escape into watercourses

Rust Fungus which discolours leaves and stems of plants

Rutting Male animals that are in a state of sexual excitement, especially deer

Shearling A young sheep after it has first been sheared and before its second shearing

Silage Fermented grass and other forage crops fed to animals

Single Farm Payment The main agricultural subsidy in the European Union

Singling Reducing the number of plants in a row

Slaughterhouse See abattoir

Slurry Liquid manure from farm livestock

Snout Nose

Sow A female pig that has given birth to a litter of piglets

Staddle Stone Two stones which make a mushroom shape to prevent mice entering a granary

Steer Castrated bull, also known as a bullock or stirk

Stallion An entire adult male horse

Stone Fruit Plums and cherries

Store/Stores Cattle or lambs being fattened for sale

Strip Squeeze first drops of milk from an udder; Strip Out: Squeeze last drops of milk

Suckler A young animal that is still drinking milk from its mother

Suckler Herd A group of cows whose calves stay with them until they are naturally weaned

Sward A stretch of grass or turf

Swath Row of grass or other plants left lying on the ground after being cut

Sway Curve of the spine

Swine Pertaining to pigs

Switch The feathery tip of an animal's tail

Tailcorn Grain left on the ground in a field after it has been harvested

Tallow The fat from animals, mainly cattle and sheep, which can be used to make candles, soap, lubricants etc.

Tassels Two pieces of hairy skin hanging from a goat's throat

Teats Where young animal drink milk from in cows, sheep etc.

Tedding Spreading cut grass to expose it to the sun in haymaking

Terminal Sire An animal which, when crossed with another breed, produces offspring for slaughter but not for reproduction

Thresh Remove the grain from the stalks of wheat, barley etc. when harvesting

Tilth Light crumbly soil suitable for sowing seeds

Tine The sharp spike on a harrow, fork or cultivator

Top Dress Apply fertiliser to a growing crop

Top Fruit Agricultural term for apples and pears

Topping Cutting weeds that have grown too long

Tramlines Tractor tracks later used for spraying to avoid damage to crops

Trash Stubble and debris left in field after crop has been harvested

Tup Another word for a ram

Udder Mammary gland with more than one teat

Vacuum Pump Device for extracting milk from animals

Veal The meat from a calf

Vernalise Use of cold weather to enable crops to develop properly

Vining Harvesting peas for freezing or canning

Volunteer An unwanted plant that has self-seeded in a field of crops

Weaner A young pig or other animal which has been weaned

Weaning When a young animal gradually ceases to rely on milk as its main food source

Wether A castrated male sheep

Wilt Disease that causes leaves to shrivel and droop

Windrow A row of grass left to dry

Winnow Removing dust or 'chaff' from grain. Part of the combining process

Withers Ridge between the shoulder blades of an animal

Zero Grazing System where grass is grown and cut to feed animals rather than allowing them to graze

Photographic Credits:

Crops: *p8 left* Birds Eye, *right* Thanet Earth; *p9* British Carrots; *p10 below right* John Hitchins; *p19 below* G's Growers Shropshire; *p30* John Hitchins; *p34 below right* Riverford; *p35* John Hitchins; *p39* Mushroom Growers Association; *p45 below right* Thanet Earth; *p49 below* John Hitchins; *p50* Leafy Salads Association; *p52 top left, p55 below right* John Hitchins; *p56 below* Vitacress Salads Ltd; *p58* Re-Gro; *p62* David Wootton Photography

Cattle: *p70* E. Matheson; *p73* Galloway Cattle Society; *p79 above* Lincoln Red Cattle Society, *below* Cogent; *p82* Pauline Stevens; *p84 below* Shelly Rogerson; *p85, p86* Museum of English Rural Life; *p87, p89* De Laval; *p91* Margaret Vale; *p96* Shelly Rogerson; *p98* Joan Lennard; *p99* Cools farm Salisbury; *p100* St Clair Shetland cattle

Pigs: *p103 top* J SR Farms Ltd, *below right* Mr & Mrs Joel, Framfield Farm; *p105 below* Derek Colbourne; *p106* Kenniford Farm Shop; *p107* Helen & Wilf Mc Sherry; *p109 above* JSR Farms Ltd, *below* Alison Shinn; *p110 above* Quarryhaed Fine Meats, *below* John Millard Hygene Pigs Ltd; *p111 below* Quarryhaed Fine Meats; *p112 below* Gillo Pedigree Pietrain Pigs; *p113 above* Mr & Mrs Joel www.framfieldfarm.co.uk, *below* Twinkle courtesy of Gren; *114 above* Hideaway Hogs Pedigree Welsh Pigs

Sheep: *p122 (2)* Balwen Welsh Mountain Sheep Society; *p124 (8)* Bleu de Maine Sheep Society, *(11)* Murdo; *p125 (13)* British Milksheep Society, *(14)* EAAP Animal Genetic Bank, *(15)* Richard Bishop Miller; *p126 (18)* Cheviot Sheep Society, *(19)* Damburgh Flock, *(20)* Mr Colburn; *p127 (22)* Dalesbred Sheep Breeders Association; *p128 (24)* Mark Coppack; *p129 (29)* French Livestock Breeds, *(30)* Melanie Davies Exmoor Society, *(31)* Louise and Peter Baber www.baber.co.uk; *p130 (33)* The Whitehall Flock Devon; *p131 (37)* John Lewis; *p132 (41)* Emma Lovegrove, *(42)* Maurice Parker, *(43)* Andrew Jones; *p133 (45)* EAAP Animal Genetic Bank, *(47)* Val Lawson; *p134 (48)* George Fell, *(49)* The Gavin Flock, *(51)* Marion Hope; *p135 (52)* Fraser Dixon, *(53)* J Hook Oxfordshire; *p137 (61)* Ian Sutherland, *(62)* J & M Kerr, *(63)* Society of Border Leicester Sheep Breeders; *p139 (69)* NSA, *(71)* John Stephenson; *p140 (72)* Teeswater Wools, *(74)* Vendeen Sheep Society, *(75)* Tecwyn Roberts; *p141 (76)* NSA; *p142 (81)* Whitefaced Woodland Society, *(83)* Clay Farm Partnership

Goats: *p145 above and p149 middle* Sue Thompson-Coon

Other Livestock: *p163* Scott Dyason of Pathfinder Ostrich Farm; *p164* Alex Smith; *p165 above* De Laval; *p166 below right* Alex Smith; *p167* Alex Smith; *p169 below and p170* Game Farmers Association

Lie of The Land: *p173* copyright David Chalmers by courtesy of Scarborough Museum; *p174* © Crown Copyright National Monuments Record *p175* Dr Paul Rainbird; *p177* Crown ©: Royal Commission on The Ancient and Historical Monuments of Wales; *p180 below* Dr Paul Rainbird; *p182 above* Kind permission of Oathill Community College

The Way We Farm: *pp157, 159, 160, 162, 163, 167, 169 and 170* John Hitchins; *p178* Rob Wilson-North; *p186 top* www.scotphoto.com

Buildings and Machines: *p204* Claas; *p210 below* JSR Farms Ltd; *p214 above* Weald and Downland Open Air Museum, *right* Sarah Daligan; *p215 top left* John Hitchins; *p221 top* Claas; *p225 below right* W & G Bruce

Wildlife: *p246 above* Alan Watson Forest Light

Every effort has been made to fulfil requirements with regard to reproducing copyright material. The author and publisher will be glad to rectify any omissions at the earliest opportunity.